UNDERSTANDING LIFE

UNDERSTANDING LIFE

ALFRED ADLER

edited and with an introduction by Colin Brett

INFORMATION & EDUCATIONAL SERVICES

Hazelden
Center City, Minnesota 55012-0176
1-800-328-0094
1-651-257-1331 (fax)
http://www.hazelden.org

Library of Congress Cataloging-in-Publication Data
Adler, Alfred, 1870–1937.
[Science of living]
Understanding life / Alfred Adler ; edited and with an introduction by Colin Brett. — 1st American ed.
p. cm.
Originally published : The science of living. New York : Greenberg, © 1929.
Includes bibliographical references and index.
ISBN: 1-56838-196-4 (pbk.)
1. Psychoanysis. 2. Psychology. I. Brett, Colin. II. Title.
BF175.A38 1998
150.19′53—dc21 97—49424
CIP

Cover design by David Spohn
Book design by Nora Koch/Gravel Pit Publications
Typesetting by Nora Koch/Gravel Pit Publications

CONTENTS

INTRODUCTION

About This Book

FIRST PUBLISHED IN ENGLISH in 1927, ten years before Alfred Adler's death, *Understanding Life* covers the main principles of Individual Psychology. This text is especially interesting to students of Adler's method because it contains numerous examples to illustrate the theoretical points made. The connecting thread throughout the book is the importance of having an understanding of society's needs and our willingness to contribute usefully wherever we can to the commonwealth. Readers will also find that common sense plays a significant role in Adler's thinking. Indeed, there is a story that, after Adler had held a lecture on his psychology, someone commented that everything he had said was common sense. "And what is wrong with common sense?" was his reply.

Adler was an inspiring speaker but unfortunately not a systematic writer. Several of the books that bear his name were not written by him but are collections of his lectures or of notes made by other people during his lectures. This is also the case with this text. Much of the charisma that carried Adler's early message to his listeners has therefore been lost to us, and in places his books may seem repetitive and superficial, lacking the refinement of phrase and clarity of structure that the writing process better facilitates. Nevertheless, the books contain flashes of insight and seemingly throwaway lines that clearly show that Individual Psychology is a subtle and eminently viable method.

In places Adler sounds judgmental and harsh. Certain groups have, in Adler's eyes, either no or low social interest, and are therefore poorly regarded. Indeed, the Adlerian view is that there is a direct relationship between an individual's lack of social interest (a form of community spirit) and the development and degree of neurosis. Two points need to be made here. As with all things, it is not a question of whether or not one has something, such as a neurosis, it is a question of how much of it one has. Second, while Individual Psychology continues to spread throughout the world and becomes increasingly recognized as a potent and pragmatic psychology, certain aspects of its theory need to be seen as products of their time, just as Adler needs to be seen against his temporal and social background. While Adler was a genius, he was not always necessarily right.

This book was first published in the United States as *The Science of Living* to provide a concise overview of Adler's main concepts and approach. The intention behind this new, revised, and updated edition is to offer a more accessible introduction to Adler that will appeal not only to Adlerian counselors, but also to students of psychology and interested laypeople. Consequently, sections of the text were reordered to improve the flow of argument, subheadings were added for greater clarity, and certain expressions and terms were updated in accordance with current English usage or modern Adlerian practice. Readers should also note that where *he, him,* or *his* is used, *she, her,* and *hers* should be understood, and vice versa. A glossary of key terms, suggestions for further reading, and an index have also been added.

Exactly how much refining and reorganization were undertaken by the editor of the first edition is not known, since the editor's name wasn't recorded. Nor have the original transcripts of Adler's talks survived, but it is hoped that this further revision process will enable Adler's great contributions to twentieth-century psychology to be appreciated by a wider audience.

Key Concepts of Individual Psychology

Individual Psychology is a system through which people can be understood. It is of particular value in the worlds of counseling and psychotherapy, education, organizational life, and self-help. It is a philosophy, a view of the future, and a way of helping us to make sense of how we and other people have become who and how we are.

Individual Psychology is a social psychology; it sees people as being fully functioning units who somehow have to cope with living together on a planet. It is indisputable that we need each other, for without each other we would not survive. Thus one of the main precepts of Individual Psychology is *social interest.* Our social interest is our active belonging to a group. We are aware of our own strengths, resources, and abilities; we are aware of society's needs; we have and use our empathy to put ourselves into our fellow human beings' situations; and we contribute to improve everybody's lot. Social interest can be summed up in the phrase "me with you" as opposed to "me against you" (which would be the Adlerian definition of neurosis). Sometimes social interest sounds like a code of conduct for do-gooders, and indeed, Adler described it as being an ideal vision for the future of humankind, rather than something that already existed. But doing good things is not "do-gooding," and social interest is open-eyed cooperation—an innate ability that can be learned and developed. Even though it is a concept for the future, it is something that we can see in aspects of our lives today to a greater or lesser extent.

Individual Psychology teaches us that we all are *goal-directed* beings; that is, we move *purposefully* through life toward goals that attract us. We have set these goals ourselves, often without our conscious realization. Goals are what motivate us; we perceive them as the best way for us to survive. In general, they are what we want or what we believe in our heart of hearts to be the best for us. Individual Psychology, then, does not regard people as being driven by the past, but rather being attracted by the future, a future that they create for themselves.

We all have a myriad of short-, medium-, and long-term goals in our lives, and all these goals will have one thing in common. This is what Adler refers to as the "long-term goal" or the "fictional final goal." It is in a way unfortunate that he uses this term, because this theme is not so much a goal as a recurrent melody in the music of our lives or a repeated master-pattern. An example of a fictional final goal might be, "I want to be good." It is final because it is the ultimate achievement of our lives, and fictional because we can never achieve it. The study of the long-term goal is called *teleology.*

Finally, where there is a goal, there is a line of movement toward it. As Adler points out, if we can clearly see this line of direction, then we can take a good guess at what the final goal must be.

This is a psychology that studies *purpose.* All behavior is seen as purposive; in other words, an Adlerian will look for the psychological gain behind what each of us is doing (thinking, feeling, and acting are all considered to be behaviors because they are things we do). When we understand the reasons for our behaviors, then we can change them; to focus on behaviors without looking behind and beyond them is the same as treating a symptom, not the cause. If the cause is unchanged, another symptom will replace the first one. Adler referred to his method as a "hard" psychology; hard in the sense that it is confrontative regarding the unknown reasons we have for what we do. It can be challenging to be revealed to oneself.

Closely connected with personal goals and purpose is the concept of *inferiority.* There is no doubt that humankind is biologically inferior to nature. We become ill or old and die. We fear the elements and have to build houses to protect ourselves. These things and countless others are greater than us, and we are therefore inferior, in a positive sense. Yet there are perceived inferiorities that are by their nature negative. One of these is the myth of social inferiority, where we believe that certain people are worse, or worth less, than other people. If we (and they) hold such a belief, even if it is not true, we (and they) will act accordingly.

On the one hand, then, our physical and intellectual inferiorities are factual and natural. As children we all feel inferior, and are so. As we grow up, however, we lose—or should lose—this sense of inferiority. We do not always do so. Many of us doubt our equal human value and have in some aspect of our lives a feeling that we are not as good as other people. As we are social beings and do not wish other people to see that we feel inferior, we try to cover this up by developing and displaying some form of superiority. We have a number of ways of doing this, one of which is overcompensation (doing something more than the situation demands). Another is deprecating others, yet another is avoiding everything that could risk our exposure. In other words, we are moving from a felt minus to a desired plus, from a feeling of not being good enough to a belief that we are indeed good enough—a natural development, and one that can be encouraged. This, in turn, means that the felt sense of inferiority is useful, as we wish to move away from it, and in doing so we develop ourselves and society. The felt minus, then, is only a problem when it hinders our progress.

We have seen above that the concept of moving toward a goal is fundamental to Individual Psychology. *Courage* is the fuel that we use to move us toward our socially useful goals. Courage is also a belief in self and can be described by the phrase "I can" as opposed to the belief that "I can't." Courage implies the willingness to do what we can, focusing on our willingness to contribute and our efforts to do so, rather than focusing on a perfect and completed product or action. Adlerian counseling and therapy can be seen as the process whereby people gain courage—a belief in themselves and their abilities. The counseling moves from a belief that "I'll give it my best shot." Being courageous—believing in ourselves—implies being independent of success and failure. Our self-worth does not depend on getting it right or being right, but on doing what we can do when the situation demands our input. Failure to an Adlerian isn't not succeeding, but rather not trying.

Encouragement, then, is seen as the development of self-esteem, a growth in the belief that "I am good enough as I am." Individual Psychology teaches that we are what we believe, that our conscious thoughts, our feelings, our emotions, and our behavior are all the products of a unique belief system that each of us holds out of our awareness. In part, our beliefs will match those held by the people around us, and this we refer to as common sense. The areas in which our belief system differs from other people's are referred to as *private logic.* On the one hand, it is my private logic that makes me who I am, makes me unique. On the other hand, it can become a source of difficulty in that it can hinder me from being a fully functioning member of society. My beliefs become the source of my inabilities.

One aspect of private logic is the "only if" beliefs I hold. Picking up the example above, I am likely to attempt a task *only if* I am likely to succeed. This shows how I restrict myself, avoid risks (which might well lead to personal growth) and keep my self-esteem at a low ebb. I act as if my private logic were real and correct. This "as if" element in our belief system helps us to create fictions about ourselves, life, and other people, according to which we then lead our lives. The purpose of Adlerian counseling and therapy is to disclose to clients their private logic, help them to understand which of their privately held beliefs are actually ideas that interfere with their daily functioning, and through a carefully planned series of actions, to lessen the exclusive quality of the private logic and help them to lead more fulfilled lives.

This is a psychology of *use,* not *possession.* Important to an Adlerian is not so much what abilities each of us has been born with or developed, but rather what we do with what we have. Similarly, what we do is more important than what we say. Adler's advice is, when in doubt "close your ears and observe": When "the lady protests too much," ask yourself why she is doing this.

Perception, or the way we see ourselves, the world, and people, is fundamental to this psychology. Adlerian counselors do not try to change life, but the way someone experiences life. The purpose of Adlerian therapy is to help clients change their perceptive frameworks, to see things differently.

Like other psychologies, Individual Psychology sometimes speaks in generalizations. Nonetheless, it stresses the uniqueness of the individual and his or her creative abilities, and therefore only gives guidelines for our thinking. Adler very wisely said, *"Alles kann immer anders sein"*—things can always be different—which prevents Adlerians from using classifications and putting their clients into fixed categories.

Adler's Work

In The Discovery of the Unconscious, *Henri Ellenberger (p. 599 ff.) divides Adler's work into six phases:*

1. *Social medicine, 1898-1909*

   Early in his career as a doctor, Adler conceived and expressed his ideas in the area of social medicine. In his *Health Book for the Tailoring Trade,* Adler explained that he wanted to show the relationship between the economic situation and disease in a given trade, and the resulting prejudice to public health. The idea behind this was that disease can be a product of society. This phase in Adler's thinking shows a move toward blending socialism with medicine. Also at this time he advocated a teaching post with a seminar for social medicine where problems of social hygiene would be explored with a view to finding their solution.
2. *The theory of organ inferiority, 1909-1911*

   While this theory was not new, Adler's contribution lay in developing a systematic theory of organ inferiority and the relating compensatory process. This concept is defined in the glossary and further discussed on pages 34–35.
3. *The theory of neurosis, 1911-1918*

   Here Adler focused on the importance of early childhood situations and was influenced by the publication of Vaihinger's *The Philosophy of the As If.* Adler used Vaihinger's concept of "fictions." Humankind lives as if certain values were facts, as if certain beliefs were true. We live as if there were an ideal norm for human activity (the "iron-clad logic of social living"). To Adler, abnormality is the degree of an individual's deviation from that fictitious norm. Neuroses are conceived as varieties of such a deviation. Referring to inferiority, Adler added the notion that feelings of inferiority can also be brought forth by purely social factors and that even when a person has an organ inferiority, the main element is the psychological reaction. In other words, our perception of the event is more important than the event itself.

4. *Individual Psychology, 1918-1925*
   During this period, the notion of community feeling *(gemeinschaftsgefuhl)* was at the fore. Also at this time, Adler stated certain basic principles of Individual Psychology, such as those previously discussed, more clearly than he had before. This showed that his pragmatic approach to human living does not pretend to go into matters very deeply, but rather provides principles and methods that enable us to gain a practical knowledge of ourselves and others. Individual Psychology is portrayed as being essentially a study of interpersonal relationships. People are never considered in an isolated situation, but in the light of their own reactions to each other.
5. *Psychotherapy and education*
   During this phase Adler developed and refined his technique of psychotherapy, which focused on helping clients to understand themselves clearly and to choose in what way and how to make changes in their lives.
6. *Later developments, 1925-1937*
   In his later writings, Adler attributed an increased importance to the creative power of the individual as being the central factor in the construction of the "life style" (see the glossary for a definition of this concept, and chapter 4 for further discussion). This creative power was also seen in the shaping of a neurosis. The striving for superiority became more significant, and private logic became defined as the opposite of community feeling or social interest. The feeling of inferiority came to be seen as no longer a neurotic symptom, but the most essential feature of a human being, and Adler emphasized a person's tendency to move from a state of inferiority to one of superiority.

Adler: A Man Ahead of His Time

Born a Hungarian citizen in 1870, Adler received his medical degree from the University of Vienna in 1895 and already had a publication to his name when he met Sigmund Freud in 1902. From 1902 to 1911, Adler belonged to the Psychoanalytic Society, of which he had been one of the first four members and president in 1910. The year 1911 was significant for Adler: He became an Austrian citizen, resigned from the Viennese Psychoanalytic Society and founded the Society for Free Psychoanalysis, which became the Society for Individual Psychology. Nineteen eleven was also the year of the major split from Freud and the year in which Adler read Vaihinger's *Philosophy of the As If,* which provided him with a new conceptual framework for his own system. During and after the First World War, Adler's socialist opinions became clear in his publications and in the way he worked on his own ideas.

The early 1920s saw him involved in institutions in which a form of therapeutic education was organized. This early form of social medicine or multiple therapy was seen as most effective, and Adler was active in no less than twenty-six schools by 1929. These institutions were abolished in Vienna in 1934, yet the idea had been born, and the concepts of group therapy and community psychiatry are clearly recognized as having their roots in Adler's thought and work. Indeed, the first day hospital and the first self-governed social therapeutic club were developed in England by Dr. Joshua Bierer, one of Adler's disciples. In the late twenties and early thirties, Adler was concerned with systematizing his ideas. He underlined the importance of our creativity in the development of our life styles, and he gave increased emphasis to the striving for superiority, or the growth principle. This is an innate movement and is a development of Adler's concept of power. Power has been grossly misrepresented as meaning power over other people. On the contrary, Adlerians mean power within self used to overcome certain aspects of self. In other words, power is a movement toward self-improvement and community enrichment.

In the last ten years of his life, Adler's development was more focused on the transpersonal. Whereas his early medical career had given birth to the concept of organ inferiority, he moved through social inferiority to a more encompassing humanistic system, which was featured in a book written with a Lutheran pastor, Dr. Ernst Jahn. The book brought together the cure of souls and Individual Psychology.

The following timeline shows other main events in Adler's life:

1870	Born in a suburb of Vienna, second son of Jewish parents
1898	Published *Health Book for Tailoring Trade*
1902	Met Sigmund Freud
1904	Became a Protestant
1910	Was president of the Viennese Psychoanalytic Society
1911	Became an Austrian citizen
1911	Resigned from the Viennese Psychoanalytic Society
1923	Spoke at the International Congress of Psychology in Oxford
1924	Became a professor at the Pedagogic Institute in Vienna
1924	Traveled and lectured in the United States
1929	Became the medical director of a Viennese clinic for the treatment of neuroses
1929	Became a lecturer at Columbia University, New York
1930	Received the title "Citizen of Vienna"
1932	Began teaching at Long Island Medical College
1934	Moved to the United States
1937	Died of a heart attack in Aberdeen on May 28

Adler's Personality

Information about Adler and his life comes to us from a variety of sources: Guy Manaster and Raymond Corsini mention an autobiographical essay; P. Bottome quotes her own experience and that of friends. This part of the introduction compares the information we have with Individual Psychology theories and makes informed guesses about Adler's personality.

Adler himself relates that he was his father's favorite child, that he felt rejected by his mother, that he once hurt another boy, that he suffered from rickets and fits of breathlessness, that he was impressed by the death of a younger brother, and that he narrowly escaped dying from a severe case of pneumonia (Ellenberger, p. 573). What might be the significance of remembering these particular events? Such a client might well be likely to seek a relationship with a woman that resembled the uneasy relationship he had with his mother. In fact, Adler married an ardent feminist and is said to have led a difficult marriage (on which his theory of the "masculine protest" is said to be based, which is defined on page 141 and discussed further on pages 76–78). We also see a tremendous awareness of illness and death, themes that recur in most of his own memories.

Indeed, Adler's first memory contains many elements of his psychology: "I remember sitting on a bench bandaged up on account of rickets, with my healthy elder brother sitting opposite me. He could run, jump, and move about quite effortlessly, while for me, movement of any sort was a strain and an effort. Everyone went to great pains to help me, and my mother and father did all that was in their power to do." While we cannot guess what the memory might mean exactly, we can assume that the themes of being an observer, having an understanding of physical inferiority, comparing oneself with others, helping people, and showing kindness are significant life themes to this person. Interesting is another of Adler's memories, which ends with the reflection: "There's another who's had a bad time at the hands of a doctor. But I shall be a real doctor." Here we can see a conclusion—a goal—that attracted Adler all his life. Two more memories bear a resemblance to key concepts of Individual Psychology. The first is where he hears a song that describes how people say one thing but do another, thus indicating an early interest in the difference between people's words and their deeds. The other memory is where he faces up to his fear of death by running through a cemetery; this parallels the importance of courage in overcoming a perceived weakness in oneself.

Adler's birth order shows that he was the second of seven children (one of whom died when Adler was four), and the middle of a subgroup of three. We could therefore expect him to have psychological features typical of a middle child: always under pressure, trying hard to compete with a bright older brother, and closely followed by a competitive younger brother. It's ironic that Adler, who competed with Sigmund Freud for most of his career in psychological medicine, had an older brother named Sigmund.

Individual Psychology in Practice

Like all other psychologies, Adlerian psychology offers a set of tools that can be put to a number of uses. In the next paragraphs we concentrate on the applications of Individual Psychology in mental health and hygiene.

The more structured approach to using Individual Psychology was systematized by Rudolf Dreikurs. This life style analysis consists of four main stages: The first phase, which continues throughout the counseling process, is called the relationship stage. This is where the counselor and client develop a mutually respectful, trusting relationship with a clear purpose and working agreement. The second phase is the collection of data, both about the client's problem itself and the purpose of the counseling process, and about the client's life style (see chapters 1 and 4). The material gathered here is generally about the family constellation and childhood memories (chapter 5). The third phase is the disclosure of the private logic, in which the counselor connects the problem with the client's belief system (chapters 2, 7, 10, and 11). The final stage is variously called "re-education," which reflects the importance of education in Individual Psychology, or "reorientation." This phase includes the growth of the client's self-esteem (encouragement) and an increased awareness of others.

A less structured and more regularly practiced approach is one in which the life style information is either offered by the client incidentally or informally requested by the counselor, who uses the information as it comes up rather than as part of a particular framework that might not suit the client and the presenting problem.

How does Individual Psychology help people to get better? Adler said, "The actual change in the nature of the patient can only be his own doing. I have found it most profitable to sit ostentatiously with my hands in my lap, fully convinced that no matter what I might be able to say on the point, the patient can learn nothing from me that he, as the sufferer, does not understand better, once he has recognized his lifeline.

"From the very beginning the consultant must try to make it clear that the responsibility for his cure is the patient's business, for as the English proverb very rightly says: 'You can lead a horse to water, but you can't make him drink.' One should always look at the treatment and the cure not as the success of the consultant, but as the success of the patient. The adviser can only point out the mistakes, it is the patient who must make the truth living." (Ansbacher 1964, p. 336)

While reference is made here to the uses of Individual Psychology in counseling and therapy, it is also widely used in education and in organizational work; the principles are the same, but the purpose and application will differ, as the following shows.

Therapeutic Education

Individual Psychology is unusual in that it is a particularly educational model of psychology, a fact that forms an integral aspect of its application to counseling and psychotherapy. Chapter 8 reflects Adler's keen personal interest in this subject.

As early as 1904 (two years after he had met Freud), Adler wrote a lengthy article in which he developed a complete theory of education (Ansbacher, 1969, p. x). In this article, "The Physician as Educator," Adler puts across four major ideas: the development of self-confidence in the child, the use of natural consequences as a disciplinary method, that a child should have no fear of the child's teacher, and that children should be educated for community living. These ideas represent the essence of what was to become Individual Psychology.

Ellenberger (p. 589) tells us that in 1920 Adler went on to found and develop institutions that were increasingly influenced by the philosophy and practice of Individual Psychology. In the same year, Adler felt that the main effort in therapeutic education should be aimed toward teachers (p. 621). He organized consultations with the parent, the child, and the teacher as part of the process. As popularity and recognition for this approach grew, other parents and teachers were invited to observe the interviews so that they could learn how the principles of Individual Psychology could improve their relationships with their own children. This structure and method is still used in Adlerian Open Family Counseling today.

A new high point in therapeutic education was reached in 1931, when an experimental school was opened in Vienna. Important features of this school's functioning included the development of community spirit, mutual aid among the children, individual consultations for pupils who needed them, and a monthly meeting of parents and teachers. Sadly, this particular school was closed in 1934, due to a change in the political climate. Nonetheless, Adler's ideas continue to have a place in education today, particularly in the United States.

For further reading we recommend

Ansbacher, Heinz L., and Rowena R. Ansbacher. *The Individual Psychology of Alfred Adler.* New York: Harper Torchbooks, 1964.

———. quoted in *Adler, The Science of Living.* New York: Anchor Books, 1969.

Ellenberger, Henri F. *The Discovery of the Unconscious.* New York: Basic Books, 1970.

Manaster, Guy, and Raymond Corsini. *Individual Psychology: Theory and Practice.* Chicago: Adler School of Professional Psychology, 1982.

I

INDIVIDUAL PSYCHOLOGY: THE SCIENCE OF LIVING

ONLY A SCIENCE that directly relates to life is really a science, said the great philosopher William James. It might also be said that in a science directly related to life, theory and practice become almost inseparable. Such a science, precisely because it models itself on the dynamics of life, becomes a science of living. These considerations apply especially strongly to the science of Individual Psychology.

Individual Psychology attempts to see individual lives as a whole and regards each single reaction, each action and impulse as an expression of an individual's attitude toward life. Such a science is of necessity practical and pragmatic, for with the aid of knowledge we can change and correct our attitudes. Individual Psychology thus not only predicts what will happen, but, like the prophet Jonah, it predicts what *might* happen so that it does *not* happen.

The science of Individual Psychology developed out of an effort to understand the mysterious creative power of life—the power expressed in the desire to develop, to strive, and to achieve, and to compensate for defeats in one area by striving for success in another. This power is *teleological*—it expresses itself in the striving for a goal, and in this striving every physical and psychological attribute cooperates. It is absurd, therefore, to study either physical or mental conditions abstractly without relating them to the individual as a whole.

For example, in criminal psychology we often pay more attention to the crime than to the criminal. But it is the criminal, not the crime, who counts, and no matter how much we contemplate the criminal act we shall never understand its nature unless we see it as an episode in the life of a particular individual. The important thing is to understand the context for the individuals involved—the goal of their lives that directs all their actions and impulses. If we can understand this goal, we can understand the hidden meaning behind each separate act—we see them as parts of a whole. And when we study the parts, provided we study them as parts of a whole, we get a better sense of the whole.

Striving toward a Goal

My interest in psychology developed out of my medical practice. Medicine provided the teleological or purposive viewpoint necessary for the understanding of psychological manifestations. In the body, all organs strive to develop toward definite goals; they have precise forms to be achieved upon maturity. Moreover, in cases where there are physical defects, we always find nature making special efforts to overcome the deficiency, or else to compensate for it by developing another organ to take over the functions of the defective one. Life always seeks survival, and the life force never yields to external obstacles without a struggle.

Now, psychological developments are analogous to organic ones. Each mind forms a conception of a goal or ideal, a means to get beyond the present state and to overcome present deficiencies or difficulties by formulating a particular aim for the future. By means of this particular aim or goal, individuals can think and feel themselves superior to present difficulties because they have future success in mind. Without this sense of a goal, individual activity would be meaningless.

All evidence points to the fact that the fixing of this goal must take place early in life, during the formative period of childhood. A prototype or model of a mature personality begins to develop at this time. We can imagine how the process takes place. Children, being weak, feel inferior and find themselves in situations they cannot bear.

Hence they strive to develop, and to do so in a direction fixed by the goal they have formulated. It is difficult to say how this goal is fixed, but it is obvious that such a goal exists and that it dominates a child's every action. Indeed, little is understood about impulse, reason, ability, or disability in early childhood. As yet there is really no key to understanding, for the direction is definitely established only after children have fixed their goals. Only when we see the direction in which a life is tending can we guess what steps will be taken in the future.

To have a goal is to aspire to be like God. To be like God is of course the ultimate goal, and educators should be cautious in attempting to educate themselves and their children to want to be like God. Children substitute a more concrete and immediate goal and look for the strongest person around them to make into their model or the embodiment of their goal. It may be the father, or perhaps the mother, or any other person. When children conceive such a goal they attempt to behave, feel, and dress like the person they have perceived to be powerful and take on all the characteristics consistent with their goal. Later on the ideal to be reached may be embodied in the doctor or the teacher, for the teacher can punish the child and thus the teacher arouses respect as a strong person, and the goal of being a doctor is fashioned around the Godlike desire of being a master over life and death. Here the goal is constructive because it can be realized through service to society.

Ways of Seeing the World

When the prototype—that early personality embodying a goal—is formed, the individual becomes oriented toward a certain direction. This enables us to predict what will happen later in life. Individuals' apperceptions are from then on likely to fall into the pattern they have established for themselves. Children will perceive situations according to personal schemes of apperception; that is to say, they will see the world through the prejudice of their goals and interests.

At four or five years of age, the prototype is already built up, and so to understand it we have to look for impressions made on children before or during that time. These impressions can be quite varied, far more varied than we can imagine from an adult's point of view.

It has been discovered that children with physical defects connect all their experiences with the functioning of the defective organ. For example, children with stomach trouble show an abnormal interest in eating, while those with defective eyesight are more preoccupied with visible things. This preoccupation is in keeping with the private scheme of apperception, which, we have said, characterizes everyone. It might be suggested, therefore, that in order to find out where a child's interest lies we need only ascertain which organ is defective; but things do not work out quite so simply. Children do not necessarily experience physical handicaps or deficiencies in the way that an external observer sees them, but will modify their experience of them by their own scheme of apperception. While organ inferiority counts as an element in the child's scheme of apperception, external observation does not necessarily give the key to the scheme of apperception.

The child sees everything in a scheme of relativity, which is unavoidable—none of us is blessed with knowledge of the absolute truth. We all make mistakes, but the important thing is that we can correct them. Such correction is easier as our personalities are forming. But when we do not correct them at that time, we may correct the mistakes later on by recalling the situation where they arose. Thus if we are confronted with the task of treating a neurotic patient, our problem is to discover not the ordinary mistakes he makes in later life, but the fundamental mistakes made early in his life when he was formulating his prototype. If we discover these mistakes, it is possible to correct them by appropriate treatment.

Individual Psychology, therefore, does not emphasize genetic inheritance. It is not what one has inherited that is important, but what one does with this inheritance in one's early years—the prototype built up in childhood. Heredity is of course responsible for inherited physical defects, but our problem there is simply to treat the specific problem and remove the child's disadvantage as much as possible.

Children with a physical disability are in a difficult situation and show marked signs of an exaggerated feeling of inferiority. At the time the prototype is being formed, they are already more interested in themselves than in others, and they tend to continue to be so later in life. Organ inferiority is far from being the only cause of mistakes in the prototype; other situations may cause the same mistakes, for example, being a spoiled or unwanted child. These situations are discussed further later in this book. Such children grow up handicapped in that they constantly fear attack and have never learned independence.

Parental Influences

Our next task is to find out the difficulties that confront individuals in their development. In the case of spoiled children, neither society nor their families can continue the pampering process indefinitely, so life's problems soon confront pampered children. At school, they find themselves in a new social institution, with a new social problem. They do not want to work or play with other children because they have not been prepared for the communal life of the school. In fact, their experiences at the prototype stage have made them afraid of such situations and make them always seek more pampering. The characteristics of such individuals are not inherited, for we can deduce them from the nature of their prototypes and goals. Because they have the particular characteristics conducive to their particular goals, it is not possible for them to have characteristics tending in any other direction.

One of the most common influences on a child's mind is the feeling of suppression brought about by a father's or mother's excessive punishment or abuse. This makes the child strive for a sense of release, and sometimes this is expressed in an attitude of psychological exclusion. Thus we find that some girls who have bad-tempered fathers avoid all men because they believe they are ill-tempered. Or boys who suffered under severe mothers may exclude women from their lives. This exclusion may of course be variously expressed: For instance, a child may simply become shy in the company of women, or he may become homosexual.[1] Such processes are not inherited but arise from the environment surrounding the child in the early years.

Children's early mistakes are costly, but despite this fact they receive little guidance. Parents often do not know or will not confess to children the results of their own experiences, and so children must follow their own line.

And while we are on the subject, it cannot be overemphasized that we gain nothing by punishing, admonishing, and preaching to children. Nothing is achieved when neither the child nor the adult is clear about what is wrong and what should be done to put it right. When children do not understand, they become sly and cowardly. Their prototypes, moreover, cannot be changed by punishment or preaching. Neither can they be changed by mere experience of life, for the experience of life is always perceived according to a personal scheme of apperception. It is only when we have access to the basic building blocks of personality that we can make any changes.

Birth Order

It is important to note that no two children, even those born in the same family, grow up in the same situation. Even in the same family, the atmosphere that surrounds individual children is quite unique. First children are initially alone and are thus the center of attention. Once a second child is born, oldest children find themselves dethroned and do not like the change of situation; they were once in

1. Adler's views on homosexuality were time-bound to his era. Most contemporary Adlerians view homosexuality as an orientation seldom chosen and likely to be genetically determined. They believe that homosexuals should be regarded with the mutual respect and equality that every human being deserves.

power and are no longer. This sense of tragedy goes into the formation of their prototypes and will re-emerge in their adult characteristics. Case histories show that such children nearly always suffer a downfall in adult life.

Another factor to be found is the different treatment meted out to boys and girls during their upbringing. Often boys are overvalued and girls are regarded as though they will accomplish little in life. Girls treated in this way may grow up hesitant and doubting themselves. Throughout life they may remain under the impression that only men are able to accomplish anything worthwhile.

The position of second children is also characteristic and individual. They are in an entirely different position than that of first children because for them there is always someone else setting the pace. Often they overtake their pacemaker, and if we look for the cause we shall find that the older children were disconcerted at having competition, and that reaction affected their development. The older children become frightened by the competition and do not do so well. They sink more and more in the estimation of their parents, who begin to appreciate the second child more and more. On the other hand, second children always have a pacemaker and are always in a race. All their characteristics reflect this peculiar position in the family. They tend to be rebellious and do not recognize power or authority.

History and legend recount numerous examples of powerful youngest children. The biblical story of Joseph is a case in point: He wanted to overcome all the others. That a younger brother was born into the family unknown to him years after he left home obviously does not alter the situation; his position remained that of the youngest. We find the same thing in many fairy tales, in which the youngest child plays a leading role. These characteristics originate in early childhood and cannot change until greater insight is attained. To help people, we must make them understand what happened in their early childhood. They must understand that the prototype they have developed may have a harmful influence on their lives.

Exploring Childhood Memories

A valuable tool for understanding the prototype and hence the nature of an individual is the study of childhood memories. All our knowledge and observations point to the fact that our memories are a factor in our prototype. An illustration will make this clear. Consider children with a physical problem—with a weak stomach, let us say. Their earliest memories will probably concern food in some way. Or take children who experienced problems because they were left-handed: Their left-handedness will likewise affect their viewpoint. A person may tell you about his mother who pampered him, or about the birth of a younger child. He may tell you how his parents beat him, how his father was bad-tempered, or how he was ridiculed or bullied at school. All such indications are valuable provided we learn the art of reading their significance.

The art of understanding childhood memories involves a high degree of empathy, the ability to identify oneself with children in their childhood situation. It is through such empathy that we can understand the unique significance in a child's life of the arrival of a younger child in the family, or the impression made on a child's mind by the abuse of an ill-tempered father.

Private Logic

If we observe a family with badly developed children, we shall see that though they may all seem to be intelligent (in the sense that if you ask a question they give the right answer), they have a strong feeling of inferiority. Intelligence, of course, is not necessarily common sense. The children may have an entirely personal—what we might term, a private—mental attitude of the sort that one finds among neurotic people. In a compulsion neurosis, for instance, patients realize the futility of their compulsive behavior but cannot stop it. Private understanding and a private language are also characteristic of the insane, who never speak in the language of common sense, which represents the height of social interest.

If we contrast the judgment of common sense with private logic, we shall find that the judgment of common sense is usually nearer the truth. We use common sense to distinguish between good and bad, and while we often make mistakes in a complicated situation, the mistakes tend to correct themselves. But those who are always looking out for their own private interests cannot distinguish between right and wrong as readily as others. In fact they often betray this inability, since all their actions are transparent to the observer.

Consider how crimes are committed. If we inquire about the intelligence, the understanding, and the motive of criminals, we shall find that they always look upon their crimes as both clever and heroic. They believe that they have achieved a goal of superiority; namely, that they have been more clever than the police and are able to get the better of others. They are thus heroes in their own minds and do not see that their actions indicate something quite different, something very far from heroic. Their lack of social interest, which makes all their activity harmful or socially useless, is connected with a lack of courage, with cowardice, but they do not know this. Those who turn to the useless side of life are often afraid of failure, darkness, and isolation; they wish to be with others. This is cowardice and should be labeled as such. Indeed, the best way to stop crime would be to convince everybody that crime is nothing but an expression of cowardice.

It is well known that some criminals, when they approach the age of thirty or forty, will change their ways. They will take a job, marry and become good citizens. Why? Consider burglars. How can forty-year-old burglars compete with twenty-year-old burglars? The latter are quicker and more powerful. Moreover, at the age of thirty or forty, criminals are forced to live differently from the way they lived before; so, because it does not bring them the things they need, crime no longer pays and they find it convenient to retire.

Another fact to be remembered in connection with criminals is that if we make punishments more severe, far from frightening the individual criminals, we merely help to reinforce their belief that they are heroes. We must not forget that criminals live in a self-centered world, a world in which one will never find true courage, self-confidence, a sense of community, or understanding of common values. It is not possible for people in this state to play a useful role in society. Neurotics seldom start a club, and this would be an impossible feat for people suffering from agoraphobia or for the criminally insane. Problem children rarely make friends, a fact for which the reason is seldom given. There is a reason, however: They rarely make friends because their early life took a self-centered direction. Their prototypes were oriented toward false goals and a private system of logic, so they followed a direction leading to the useless side of life.

The Importance of Social Interest

The concept of social interest or social feeling is a vital one. It is the most important part of our education, of our treatment, and of our cure. Only people who are courageous, self-confident, and at home in the world can benefit from both the problems and the advantages of life. They are never afraid. They know that there are always difficulties in life, but they also know that they can overcome them. They are prepared for all life's problems, which are invariably of a social nature.

The three types of children we have mentioned—those who are affected by a physical disability, pampering, or a difficult family situation—develop a prototype with a lesser degree of social interest. They do not have the mental attitude necessary for the solution of life's difficulties. Feeling defeated, they develop a mistaken attitude toward the problems of life. Our task in treating such patients is to encourage what I describe as "useful" social behavior and a positive, or "useful" attitude toward life and society.

Lack of social interest tends to orient people toward the negative or "useless" side of life.

Individuals who seriously lack social interest may become delinquents, criminals, alcoholics, or mentally ill. Our problem in their case is to find a means to influence them to adopt useful and constructive behavior patterns and to make them interested in others. It may be said that our so-called Individual Psychology is actually a social psychology.

Feelings and Emotions

The next step in the science of living lies in the study of feelings. Not only does the adoption of a goal affect individual characteristics, physical movements, and expressions, it also dominates the life of the feelings. It is a remarkable thing that individuals always try to justify their attitudes by an appeal to their feelings. Thus if individuals are keen to do good work, we will find this idea magnified and playing a dominant role in their emotional life. Individuals' feelings always agree with their viewpoint of their task: The feelings strengthen their assumptions. We always do what we would do anyway, and our feelings are simply an accompaniment to our acts.

We can see this quite clearly in dreams, the study of which is perhaps one of the greatest achievements of Individual Psychology. Every dream has a purpose, although this was never clearly understood before. The purpose of a dream, in general, is to create a certain feeling or emotion, which in turn furthers the object of the dream. We dream in the way that we would like to behave. Dreams are an emotional rehearsal of plans and attitudes for our waking behavior—a rehearsal, however, for which the actual play may never come off. In this sense dreams are deceptive, the emotional imagination gives us the thrill of action without the action.

This characteristic is also found in our waking life. We always have a strong inclination to deceive ourselves emotionally; we always want to persuade ourselves to go the way dictated by our prototypes, as they were formed in early childhood.

The General Approach

This sums up the approach of Individual Psychology, a science that has traveled a long way in a new direction. There are many psychologies and psychiatries, and no one psychologist believes that the others are right. Perhaps the reader, too, should not rely on belief and faith; let the reader study and compare.

II
THE INFERIORITY COMPLEX

Consciousness and Unconsciousness

THE USE OF THE TERMS *consciousness* and *unconsciousness* to designate distinct entities is considered incorrect in Individual Psychology. The conscious and the unconscious minds work together in the same direction and are not in opposition or in conflict, as is so often believed. What is more, there is no definite line of demarcation between them. The important thing is to discover the purpose of their joint efforts. It is impossible to decide what is conscious and what is not until the whole context has been understood. This is revealed in the prototype, that pattern of life that we analyzed in the last chapter.

A case history will serve to illustrate the intimate connection between the conscious and unconscious life. A married man, forty years old, suffered from a constant desire to jump out of the window. He was always struggling against this desire, but aside from this problem he was quite healthy. He had friends, a good job, and lived happily with his wife. His case is inexplicable except in terms of a collaboration between consciousness and unconsciousness.

Consciously, he had the feeling that he must jump out of a window. Nonetheless he carried on with his life, and in fact never even attempted to jump out of a window. The reason for this phenomenon is that there was another side to his life, a side in which a struggle against his desire to commit suicide played an important part. As a result of the collaboration between this unconscious side of his being and his consciousness, he came out victorious. In fact, in terms of his life style—to use a term we will discuss in more detail in a later chapter—he was a conqueror who had attained the goal of superiority.

The reader might ask: How could this man feel superior when he had this conscious longing *to commit suicide?* The answer is that there was something in him that was fighting a battle against his suicidal tendency. His success in this battle made him a conqueror and a superior being. To an objective observer it is clear that the man's struggle for superiority was conditioned by his weakness, as is often the case with people who in one way or another feel inferior. But the important thing is that in his private battle his striving for superiority, his striving to live and to conquer, came out ahead of his sense of inferiority and desire to die—and this despite the fact that the latter was expressed in his conscious life and the former in his unconscious life.

Let us see if the development of this man's prototype bears out our theory; let us analyze his childhood memories. At an early age, we learn, he disliked school. He feared other boys and wanted to run away from them. Nonetheless, he mustered all his determination to stay and face them. Here we can already perceive an effort on his part to overcome his weakness: He faced his problem and conquered it.

If we analyze our patient's character, we see that his one aim in life was to overcome fear and anxiety. In this aim his conscious ideas cooperated with his unconscious ones to form a united whole. Now, someone who does not view the human being as a unity might see this patient only as an ambitious person who wanted to struggle and fight but who was at bottom a coward. This would be a misplaced view, however, since it would not take into account all the facts in the case and interpret them with regard to the fundamental unity of a human life. Our whole psychology, and all our attempts to understand individuals, are futile and useless unless we acknowledge that the human being is a unity. If we presuppose two sides to each person, having no relation to one another, it is impossible to see life as a coherent entity.

Our Social Relationships

In addition to regarding an individual's life as a unity, we must also examine it in its context of social relationships. When human beings are first born they are weak, and their weakness makes it necessary for others to care for them. The pattern of children's lives cannot be understood without reference to the people who look after them and who compensate for their weakness. Children have interlocking relationships with their mothers and families that could never be understood if we confined our analysis to children as separate entities. Children's individualities are made up of more than their physical individuality; they involve a whole network of social relationships.

What applies to children applies to all of us, to a certain extent. The weakness that makes it necessary for children to live in a family group parallels the weakness that drives people to live in communities. Everyone feels inadequate in certain situations. They feel overwhelmed by the difficulties of life and incapable of meeting them single-handedly. Hence one of the strongest tendencies in humanity is the movement to form groups to live as members of a community and not as isolated individuals. This social life has without doubt been a great help to us in overcoming our feelings of inadequacy and inferiority.

In animals, too, those of the weaker species always live in groups so that their combined powers might help to meet their individual needs. Thus a herd of buffalo can defend themselves against wolves, whereas one buffalo alone would find this impossible. On the other hand, gorillas, lions, and tigers can live in isolation because nature has given them the means of self-protection. A human being does not have the animals' great strength, their claws, or their teeth, and so cannot live apart; the beginning of social life lies, therefore, in the weakness of the individual.

Because of this, we cannot expect to find that the abilities of all human beings are equal. But a society that is organized appropriately will support the varying abilities of the individuals who make it up.

This is an important point to grasp, since otherwise we would be led to suppose that individuals have to be judged entirely on their inherited abilities. As a matter of fact, individuals who might be deficient in certain faculties if they lived in an isolated condition could well compensate for their shortcomings in a well-organized society that encouraged them to contribute their particular skills.

Let us suppose that we inherit our individual insufficiencies. If so, it becomes the aim of psychology to help people to live well with others, to decrease the effect of their natural setbacks. The history of social progress is the story of how people have cooperated to overcome deficiencies and problems.

Language and Communication

Everybody realizes that language is a social invention, but few people acknowledge that individual deficiency was the mother of that invention. This truth, however, is illustrated in the early behavior of children. When their desires are not satisfied, they want to gain attention and they try to do so by some sort of language. If children did not need to gain attention, they would not try to speak at all. In the first few months of life, the child's mother supplies everything that the child wishes, before speech develops. There are cases on record of children who did not speak until they were six years of age because it was never necessary for them to do so.

The same truth is illustrated in the case of a particular child of parents who were hearing and speech impaired. When he fell and hurt himself he cried, but he cried without noise. He knew that noise would be useless, as his parents could not hear him. Therefore, he made the appearance of crying to gain the attention of his parents, but it was silent.

We see, therefore, that we must always look at the whole social context of the facts we study. We must look at the social environment to understand the particular "goal of superiority" individuals choose, and their particular social problem. Individual Psychology therefore examines all problems against the background in which they occur. Many people have difficulty adjusting to society because they find it impossible to make normal contact with others by means of language. People with speech impediments are an example. If we examine people with this problem we shall see that from childhood they were not well adjusted socially; they rarely wanted to join in activities or to have friends or companions. Language development needs association with others, but since these people were unwilling to associate, their speech problems continued. There are really two impulses in people with speech problems: one that makes them want to associate with others and another that drives them to seek isolation.

Many adults who do not live a life in which social contact plays an important part find they cannot speak in public and tend to have stage fright. This is because they regard their audiences as enemies. They have a feeling of inferiority when confronted by a seemingly hostile and dominating audience. Only when people trust themselves and their audience can they speak well, and only then will they not have stage fright.

Social Training

The feeling of inferiority and the problem of social training are thus intimately connected. The feeling of inferiority arises from social maladjustment, while social training is the basic method by which we can all overcome our feelings of inferiority.

There is also a direct connection between social training and common sense. When we speak of common sense, we have in mind the pooled intelligence of the social group. On the other hand, as mentioned in the last chapter, people who use a private language and a private understanding demonstrate that other people, social institutions, and social norms hold no appeal for them. And yet it is through these things that the road to their salvation lies.

In working with such people our task is to make community life appeal to them. Nervous people always feel justified if they show goodwill, but more than goodwill is needed. We must teach them that it is what they actually accomplish, what they finally give, that matters to society.

While the feeling of inferiority and the striving for superiority are universal, it would be a mistake to regard this as an indication that everyone is equal. There are differences in bodily strength, in health, and in external circumstances. For that reason individuals in apparently similar conditions make different mistakes. If we examine children, we see that there is no single absolutely fixed and right manner for them to respond to their circumstances. They respond in their individual ways. They strive toward a better life style, but they all strive in their own way, making their own mistakes, and using their own approximations of success.

Overcoming Limitations

Let us analyze some of the variations and peculiarities individuals can demonstrate. Let us take, for example, left-handed children. There are children who may never know that they are left-handed because they have been so carefully trained in the use of the right hand. At first they are clumsy with their right hand, and they are scolded and criticized.

Left-handed children can be recognized in the cradle because their left hands move more than their right. In later life, they may feel burdened by the weakness of their right hand, and in the effort to overcome this problem often they develop a greater interest in drawing, writing, and so on. This is a great advantage in developing latent artistic talent and ability, and children in such a position are often ambitious and fight to overcome their limitations. Sometimes, however, if the struggle is a serious one, they may become envious of others and thus develop a greater feeling of inferiority. Through constant struggling, children may turn into combative adults, always striving with the fixed idea in mind that they ought not be awkward and found wanting.

Children strive, make mistakes, and develop in different ways according to the prototypes they formed in the first four or five years of life. Each of them will have a different goal. Some may want to be painters, while others may wish themselves away from this world in which they are uncomfortable. We may know how they can overcome their weakness, but they do not, and all too often the facts are not explained to them in the right way.

Many children have imperfect eyes, ears, lungs, or stomachs, and we find their interest stimulated in the direction of the imperfection. An interesting example of this is seen in the case of a man who suffered from attacks of asthma only when he came home from the office at night. He was forty-five, married, and had a good job. He was asked why the attacks always occurred after he came home from work. He explained, "You see, my wife is very materialistic whereas I am idealistic, so we do not always agree. When I come home I would like to relax, to enjoy myself quietly at home, but my wife wants to go out and so she complains about having to stay at home. Then I get into a bad temper and start to suffocate."

Why did this man suffocate? Why did he not, for example, vomit? The fact is that he was simply being true to his prototype. It seems that as a child he had to be bandaged for some weakness and this tight binding affected his breathing and made him very uncomfortable. He had a nurse, however, who liked him and would sit beside him and console him. All her interest focused on him rather than herself. Consequently, she gave him the impression that she would always amuse and console him. When he was four years old the nurse went away to a wedding, and he accompanied her to the station, crying very bitterly. After the nurse had left he said to his mother, "The world no longer has any interest for me now that my nurse has gone away."

Hence we see him in adulthood just as he was in the early years when he was forming his prototype: looking for an ideal person who will always amuse him and console him and be interested solely in him. His problem lay not in insufficient oxygen, but in the fact that he was not being amused and consoled at all times. Naturally, to find a person who will always amuse you is not easy. He always wanted to control every situation, and to a certain degree this desire helped him when he succeeded. Thus when he started to suffocate—when his wife stopped wanting to socialize or go to the theater—he had obtained his "goal of superiority."

On the conscious level this man was always right and proper, but subconsciously he was driven by the desire to be the conqueror. He wanted to make his wife what he called idealistic instead of materialistic. We should suspect similar behavior of a man of motives at variance with those on the surface.

Similarly, we often see children with poor eyesight take greater interest in visual things. It is not uncommon for poets and painters to have trouble with their eyes. Gustav Freitag, for example, was a great poet with poor, astigmatic eyesight who accomplished much. He said about himself, "Because my eyes were different to those of other people, it seems that I was compelled to train and use my imagination. I do not know that this has helped me to be a great writer, but in any case as a result of my eyesight I can see better in my imagination that others can in reality."

If we examine the personalities of geniuses, we often find poor eyesight or some other physical disadvantage. Even the gods of mythology had some deficiency such as blindness in one or both eyes. That there are geniuses who, even though nearly blind, are still able to understand better than others the differences in lines, tones, and colors shows what can be done with affected children if their problems are properly understood.

Some people are especially interested in food. Because of this they are always discussing what they can and cannot eat. Usually such people have had digestive problems when they were young and so have developed greater interest in food than others. They had probably had an anxious mother who constantly told them what they could or could not eat. Such individuals then have to make an effort to overcome their stomach problems, and they become vitally interested in what they will have for breakfast, lunch, or dinner. As a result of their preoccupation with food, they sometimes become very good cooks or experts on dietary matters.

At times, however, a weakness of the stomach or the intestines causes people to look for a substitute for eating. Sometimes this substitute is money, and such people may become miserly or great money financiers. They often strive extremely hard to accumulate money, training themselves for this purpose day and night. They never stop thinking of their business—a fact that may sometimes give them a great advantage over others in similar circumstances. Furthermore, it is interesting to note that we often hear of rich people suffering from stomach complaints.

Let us remind ourselves at this point of the importance of the connection between body and mind. A certain defect in different people does not always have the same consequences; there is no necessary cause-and-effect relationship between a physical deficiency and a poor way of life. The physical condition can often be effectively treated, or at least alleviated, but it is not the defect itself that brings bad results; it is the patient's attitude toward it that is responsible. That is why, for the Individual psychologist, mere physical causality does not exist, but only mistaken attitudes toward physical conditions. Also, that is why the Individual psychologist seeks to encourage the overcoming of the feeling of inferiority during the development of the prototype.

Sometimes we encounter people who seem permanently impatient because they cannot wait to overcome their difficulties. Whenever we see someone constantly on the go, with a strong temper and moods, we can conclude that they have a powerful feeling of inferiority. People who believe they can overcome their difficulties will not be impatient.

Arrogant, impertinent, quarrelsome children also indicate a great feeling of inferiority. It is our task in their case to look for the reasons for the difficulties they are trying to overcome in order to prescribe appropriate treatment. We should never criticize or *punish* mistakes in the life style of the prototype.

We can recognize these characteristics within the prototype among children in particular ways—in unusual interests, in scheming and striving to outdo others, and in pursuing the goal of superiority. There are types that do not trust their own abilities to act and express themselves, preferring to exclude other people as far as possible. They avoid new situations and try to stay in the little circle in which they feel secure. In school, in employment, in society, and in marriage they do the same, always hoping to accomplish much in their own little sphere in order to arrive at a goal of superiority. We find this trait quite often among people who forget that to accomplish anything worthwhile, one must be prepared to face whatever life throws at us. Individuals who rule out certain situations and certain people as impossible can only use private logic to justify themselves, and this is not enough. People need the fresh air of social contact and common sense to live a healthy life.

People all face different requirements in their lives. If writers, for example, want to achieve something in their work, they cannot always go off to lunch or dinner with others, for they need to be alone for long periods of time in order to collect their ideas. But they must also grow through social interaction because this contact is an important part of their development. And so when we encounter such people we must remember their two requirements, and also that they can be either socially useful or useless. We should therefore look carefully to see the difference between useful and useless behavior.

Feelings of Inferiority

The key to the social process is that people are always striving to find a situation in which they can excel. Thus, children who have a strong feeling of inferiority want to exclude bigger children and play with the younger or weaker ones whom they can dominate. This is an abnormal and pathological expression of the feeling of inferiority, for it is important to realize that it is not the sense of inferiority itself that matters but its degree and expression.

An abnormal feeling of inferiority has acquired the name of "inferiority complex." But *complex* is not the correct word for a feeling that permeates the whole personality. It is more than a complex; it is almost a disease whose severity varies under different circumstances. Thus we sometimes do not notice someone's feeling of inferiority when they are at work because they feel sure of their ability, but they may not be sure of themselves in the company of others, particularly in their relations with the other sex, and there we are able to discover their true psychological situation.

Mistakes are more evident in a tense or difficult situation. When an individual is in a difficult or new situation, the prototype appears more clearly, a difficult situation being more often than not a new one. That is why, as we said in the first chapter, the expression of a person's degree of social interest becomes evident in a new social situation.

When we send children to school we may observe their social interest in seeing whether they mix with their fellow pupils or avoid them. If they respond to other children only conditionally or hesitantly, we must be on the lookout for the same characteristics being revealed later on in society and marriage.

There are many people who say, "I would do that in this way," "I would take that job," "I would take on that person, *but*. . . !" All such statements indicate a strong feeling of inferiority, and if we interpret them in this way we get a new insight into certain emotions, such as doubt. A person who feels in doubt usually remains in doubt and accomplishes nothing.

The psychologist can often see hesitations and contradictions in people, which may be considered signs of a feeling of inferiority, but we must also take into account the physical movements of the subjects. Their approach, or way of dealing with other people, may be poor; perhaps they approach hesitantly or with an awkward bodily posture. This hesitation will often be expressed in other situations in life. Many people habitually take one step forward and one step backward—quite literally.

Our whole task is to train people away from this hesitant attitude. The proper treatment is to encourage them, never to discourage them. We must make them understand that they are capable of facing difficulties and solving the problems of life. This is the only way to build self-confidence, and this is the only way the feeling of inferiority can be treated.

III
THE SUPERIORITY COMPLEX

The Goal of Superiority

In the last chapter we discussed the inferiority complex and its relationship with the general feeling of inferiority that all of us share and struggle against. Now we turn to its complement, the superiority complex.

We have seen how every characteristic of an individual's life is expressed in a transition—in a progression. Thus the characteristic may be said to have a past and a future. The future is tied up with our striving and our goal, while the past represents the state of inferiority or inadequacy that we are trying to overcome. That is why, in the case of an inferiority complex, we are interested in its beginning, while in a superiority complex, we are more interested in its progression, in the transition itself. Moreover, the two complexes are naturally related. We should not be astonished if, in cases where we see an inferiority complex, we also find a hidden superiority complex. On the other hand, if we inquire into a superiority complex and study its continuity, we can always find a more or less concealed inferiority complex. We do not strive to be superior and to succeed if we do not feel a certain deficiency in our present condition.

The striving for superiority never ceases. It is essential to the mind, to the psyche of the individual. As we said, life is the attainment of a goal or ideal form, and it is the striving for superiority that sets it in motion. If we look at lazy children and see their lack of activity, their lack of interest in anything, we may say that they do not seem to be progressing in any direction. Nonetheless, we find in them a desire to be superior, a desire that makes them say, "If I were not so lazy, I could be president." They are progressing and striving conditionally, so to speak. They hold a high opinion of themselves and take the view that they could accomplish much if only. . . ! This is self-deception, of course. It is fiction, but as we all know, humanity is very often satisfied with fiction. And this is especially true of people who lack courage. They do not feel strong, and so they always make detours around difficulties, always trying to escape them. Through this process of escape and evasion they maintain a feeling of being much stronger and more clever than they really are.

Avoiding Real Solutions

Children who steal suffer from a feeling of superiority. They believe they are deceiving others, that others do not know they are stealing, and that they have become richer with little effort. This same feeling is very pronounced among criminals who have the idea that they are heroes.

We have already spoken of this trait from another point of view, as a manifestation of a private logic. It is not common or social sense. If murderers think themselves heroic, that is a private idea. They are in fact lacking in courage, since they want to arrange matters in a way that avoids the necessity of applying real solutions to the problems of life. Criminality is thus the expression of a superiority complex, not of a fundamental or original wickedness.

We see similar symptoms appearing in neurotic people. For example, they may suffer from insomnia and so do not feel strong enough to fulfill the demands of their jobs on the following day. Because of their sleepless nights they feel they should not be required to work, because they are not up to completing the tasks they should accomplish. "What could I not achieve, if I could only get some sleep!" they wail.

We see this also among depressed people suffering from anxiety. Their anxiety turns them into tyrants over others; they use it to rule others, for they must always have people around them, they must be accompanied wherever they go, and so on. Their companions are made to live their whole lives in accordance with the needs and demands of the depressed person.

Depressed or ill people are always the center of attention in a family. In them we see the power wielded by the inferiority complex. They complain that they feel weak, are losing weight, and so on, but often they are the strongest of all in that they dominate the healthy members of the family. This should not surprise us, for in our culture weakness can be quite a powerful weapon.

Superiority and Inferiority

Let us study the connection between the superiority complex and inferiority. For example, if we study problem children with superiority complexes—children who are impertinent and arrogant—we shall find that they always want to appear bigger than they are. We know how children with temper tantrums try to control others. Why are they so demanding and impatient? Because they are not sure they are strong enough to attain their goal—they feel inferior. It is as if they were constantly on tiptoes in an effort to appear bigger than they really are and thus to gain success, pride, and superiority.

We have to find methods of treatment for such children. They act in that way because they do not understand the natural order of things. We should not censure them, but in a friendly manner explain to them the commonsense point of view and help them gradually to understand it.

If people show off it is only because they feel inferior and do not feel strong enough to compete with others in a more positive way. They are not in harmony with society. They are not socially well adjusted and do not know how to solve the social problems of life. We usually find that there was a struggle between such people and their parents and teachers during their childhood.

We see the same combination of inferiority and superiority complexes in neurotic illnesses. Neurotics often express their sense of superiority but do not acknowledge their inferiority complex. The case history of a girl suffering from compulsion neurosis is very illuminating in this regard.

This young girl was close to her older sister, who was charming and popular. This fact is significant, for if one person in a family is outstanding in some way, the others will suffer. This is always so, whether the favored individual is the father, one of the children, or the mother. This creates a difficult situation for the other members of the family, and sometimes they feel they cannot bear it.

The girl in question grew up without the favored status of her sister and felt restricted. If she had been interested in other people and had understood what we now understand, she could have followed another path. But she was always suffering from the tension of an inferiority complex caused by comparing herself with her preferred sister.

When she was twenty her sister married, and so she began to seek marriage herself in order to compete with her sister. She was drifting further and further from the healthy, useful side of life. She began to develop the idea that she was a wicked person and then the notion that she possessed magic power that could send people to hell.

We see this feeling of magic power as an expression of a superiority complex, but she complained about having this "gift," just as we sometimes hear rich people complain of how hard a fate it is to be rich. Not only did she feel that she had the godlike power to send people to hell, but at times she got the impression that she could and ought to save these people. By means of this fictitious system, she assured herself that she possessed a power higher than her sister's. Only in this way could she overcome her sister. And so she kept complaining that she had this power, for the more she complained about it the more plausible it would seem that she actually possessed it. Only by complaining could she feel happy with her lot.

The older sister had been very much favored, for at one time she was the only child and much pampered. Three years later the arrival of the younger sister changed the whole situation for the older girl. Formerly she had always been alone, the center of attention. Now she was suddenly thrown out of this position, and as a result she became an aggressive child. But there can be aggression only where there are weaker companions, and aggressive children are not really courageous—they fight only weaker adversaries. If there is no opportunity for this, children may become peevish instead, and in either case are therefore likely to be less appreciated at home.

The older child then felt she was not as dearly loved as before and saw this as a confirmation of her view about the younger child. She considered her mother the most guilty person, inasmuch as it was she who brought the new baby into the home. Thus we can understand her directing her attacks toward her mother.

The baby, of course, had to be watched and cared for, as all babies do, and was thus in a favorable position. She did not need to exert herself; she did not need to fight. She grew up as a sweet, soft, and dearly loved creature—the center of attention. Sometimes virtue, in the form of sweetness and obedience, may conquer!

Now let us analyze this sweetness and consider whether it was on the useful side of life or not. We may suppose that a child will be amenable and tractable only as long as she is pampered. When pampered children go to school, they are no longer in a favorable situation. From that moment on we see them adopting a hesitant attitude toward life.

So it was with this younger sister. She began to learn to sew, to play the piano, and so on, but in each case, after a short time she dropped her efforts to learn. She also began to lose interest in society, no longer liked to go out, and suffered from depression. She felt herself overshadowed by her older sister, who had a more agreeable personality. Her hesitancy made her become weaker and caused a deterioration in her character.

Later in life she hesitated in choosing a career and never finished any training. She also hesitated in love and marriage, despite her desire to compete with her sister. When she reached thirty, she decided to marry a man who was suffering from tuberculosis. Her parents naturally opposed this choice. In this case, she did not find it necessary to hesitate, for her parents prohibited the marriage.

A year later she married a man thirty-five years her senior. We often find an expression of an inferiority complex in the selection of a much older person as a partner, or in the selection of a person who is not free to marry. There is always a suspicion of cowardice when there are obvious hindrances. But because this girl had not justified her feeling of superiority through marriage, she found another way of doing so. She began to insist that the most important thing in this world was cleanliness. She had to wash herself all the time, she said. If anybody or anything touched her, she had to wash again. In this way she became wholly isolated.

Now this all seems like an inferiority complex, but the girl felt herself to be the only clean person in the world and was continually criticizing and accusing others because they did not have her obsession with washing. She had always wanted to be superior, and now in her fictitious way she was. She was the cleanest person in the world. So we see that her inferiority complex had developed into a superiority complex, very distinctly expressed.

Self-Interest

So long as people are interested not only in themselves but in others, they will solve the problems of life satisfactorily. But if they develop an inferiority complex, they find themselves living, as it were, in enemy territory, always looking out for their own interests rather than for those of others, and thus not having any sense of community. They approach the social problems of life with an attitude that is not conducive to their solution, and so, lacking success, they turn to the useless side of life. They feel relieved at being supported by others and not having to solve problems.

It seems to be a characteristic of human nature that when individuals—either children or adults—feel excessively weak, they cease to be interested in others but strive only for superiority. As long as people strive for personal superiority and temper their efforts with social interest, they can accomplish some good. But if they lack social interest, they are not prepared to solve life's problems.

We see the same phenomenon in megalomaniacs who believe themselves to be Jesus Christ or other great leaders. Such people play their roles almost as if they were true. They are isolated in life, and we shall find, if we go back to their pasts, that they felt painfully inferior and that, in compensation, they developed a superiority complex.

There is the case of a boy of fifteen who was committed to a mental hospital because of his hallucinations. At that time, before the First World War, he fancied that the emperor of Austria was dead. This was not true, but he claimed that the emperor had appeared to him in a dream demanding that he lead the Austrian army against the enemy. And he was a young boy! He would not be convinced of his error about the emperor's death, even when he was shown newspapers reporting on the emperor's activities. He insisted that the emperor was dead and had appeared to him in a dream.

At that time Individual Psychology was trying to find out the importance of sleeping positions in indicating a person's feeling of superiority or inferiority. Some people lie curled up in bed, covering their heads with the covers. This expresses an inferiority complex. Can we believe such people to be courageous? When we see people who stretch out straight, on the other hand, can we believe them weak in life? It has also been observed that people who sleep on their stomachs tend to be stubborn and aggressive.

This boy was observed in an attempt to find a correlation between his waking behavior and his sleeping positions. It was found that he slept with his arms crossed on his chest, like some caricature of Napoléon. Often, pictures show Napoléon with his arms in such a position.

The next day the boy was asked, "Who does this position remind you of?"

He answered, "My teacher."

The discovery was a little disturbing, until it was suggested that the teacher might resemble Napoléon. This proved to be the case. Moreover, the boy had loved his teacher and wanted to be like him.

He longed to enter the teaching profession, but for lack of funds to pay for an education, his family had to put him to work in a restaurant. There the customers had all derided him because he was small. He could not bear this and wanted to escape from this feeling of humiliation, but he escaped to the useless side of life.

We can understand what happened in the case of this boy. In the beginning he had an inferiority complex because he was small, but he was constantly striving for superiority. He wanted to be a teacher, but because he was blocked from attaining this goal he found another goal of superiority by making a detour to the useless side of life. He became superior in sleep and in hallucinations.

Boasting and Cowardice

The goal of superiority may be pursued by either useless or useful activity. If people are benevolent, for instance, it may mean one of two things: It may mean that they are socially well adjusted and want to help, or it may simply mean that they want to show off.

The psychologist meets many people whose main goal is to show off and boast. A similar tendency may be seen in the behavior of animals: the tendency to claim easy success. New York newspapers once reported how some schoolteachers disturbed a burglar after he broke into their home. He had an interesting discussion with them. The burglar told the women they did not know how difficult it was to earn a living in ordinary, honest occupations; it was much easier to be a burglar than to work. This man had escaped to the useless side of life, but by taking this road he had developed a certain superiority complex. He felt stronger than the women, particularly since he was armed and they were not. But did he realize that he was a coward? On the contrary, he thought himself a hero.

Some types turn to suicide and seek to throw off the whole world with all its difficulties. They do not seem to care for life and so feel superior, although they are really cowards. We see that a superiority complex is a secondary development. It is a compensation for the inferiority complex. We must always try to find an organic connection—the connection that may seem to be a contradiction but which is quite in accordance with human nature, as we have already shown. Once we find this connection, we are in a position to treat both the inferiority and superiority complexes.

Healthy Ambition

We should not conclude the general subject of inferiority and superiority complexes without saying a few words about the relationship between these complexes and normal impulses, for everyone, as we have said, has a feeling of inferiority. But the feeling of inferiority is not a disease, it is a stimulant to healthy, normal development. It becomes a pathological condition only when the sense of inadequacy overwhelms individuals, and instead of stimulating them to useful activity, makes them depressed and incapable of development.

The superiority complex is one of the ways people who feel inferior try to escape from their difficulties. They persuade themselves that they are superior when they are not, and this false success compensates them for the state of inferiority that they cannot bear.

Normal people do not have a superiority complex; they do not even have a sense of superiority. They have ambition to be successful, but so long as this striving is constructively expressed, it does not lead to false values, which lie at the root of mental illness.

IV

THE LIFE STYLE

Recognizing Life Style

A PINE TREE GROWING in the valley grows differently from one on top of a mountain. The same kind of tree has two distinct life styles. Its style on top of the mountain is different from its style when growing in the valley. The life style of a tree is the individual expression of a tree molding itself to its environment. We recognize a style when we see it set against a background different from the one we would expect, for then we realize that every tree has its own life pattern and its growth is not merely a mechanical reaction to the environment.

It is much the same with human beings. We see the life style under certain conditions, and it is our task to analyze its exact relation to existing circumstances, inasmuch as the mind changes with any alteration in the environment. As long as people are in a favorable situation, we cannot see their life styles clearly. In new situations, however, where they are confronted with difficulties, the life styles appear clearly and distinctly. A trained psychologist could perhaps understand the life style of a human being even while in a favorable situation, but it becomes apparent to everybody when the subject is put into unfavorable or difficult circumstances.

Life is something more than a game, and it is always full of difficulties. There are, inevitably, circumstances in which human beings find themselves confronted with problems, and it is while subjects are confronted with these difficulties that we must study them and find out their different responses and characteristic features. As we have said, the life style is a unity because it has grown out of the difficulties of early life and out of the striving for a goal.

But we are interested not so much in the past as in the future, and to understand someone's future we must understand his life style. Even if we understand instincts, stimuli, drives, and so on, we cannot predict what will happen. Some psychologists try to reach conclusions based on their observation of instinctive behavior or evidence of trauma, but on closer examination it will be found that all these elements presuppose a consistent life style. Thus, whatever stimulus is received, it only serves to reinforce a life style.

We have seen how human beings with physical deficiencies, because they face difficulties and feel insecure, suffer from a feeling of inferiority. But as human beings cannot endure this for long, the inferiority feeling stimulates them to action, as we have seen, and this results in the formulation of a goal. Individual Psychology first called the consistent movement toward this goal a "plan of life," but because this name sometimes led to misunderstanding it is now called the life style.

Because individuals have life styles, it is sometimes possible to predict their future just by talking to them and asking questions. It is like looking at the fifth act of a drama, where all the mysteries are solved. We can make predictions in this way because we know the usual phases, difficulties, and questions of life. Thus, from experience and the knowledge of a few facts we can predict what will happen to children who always keep away from others, who are looking for support, who are pampered, and who hesitate in approaching new situations. What happens in the case of people whose goal is to be always supported by others? Hesitating, they stop seeking or escape from the solution to the questions of life. We know that they can hesitate, stop, or escape, because we have seen the same thing happen a thousand times. We know that they do not want to cope alone but want to be pampered, to stay away from the basic problems of life, or occupy themselves with irrelevant things rather than struggle with important matters. They lack social interest, and as a result may develop into problem children, neurotics, criminals, or become suicidal—the final escape. All these things are now better understood than formerly.

We realize, for instance, that in looking for the life style of a human being we may use a "normal" life style as a basis for measurement. We use the socially well-adjusted human being as a reference, and we can then measure variations from this reference.

The "Normal" Life Style

At this point, perhaps it would be helpful to show how we determine the "normal" life style and how we go on from there to recognize mistakes and peculiarities.

Human beings cannot be divided into types because every human being has an individual life style. Just as one cannot find two leaves of a tree that are absolutely identical, one cannot find two human beings who are absolutely alike. Nature is so rich, and the possibilities for stimuli are so numerous, that it is not possible for two people to be identical. If we speak of types, therefore, it is only as an intellectual device to identify the similarities between individuals. We can draw clearer conclusions if we postulate an intellectual classification and study its special peculiarities, but in doing so we do not commit ourselves to using the same classification at all times; we use the classification that is most useful for bringing out a particular similarity. People who take types and classifications too seriously tend to put people in pigeonholes and then fail to see how they can be put into any other classification.

An illustration will make my point clear. When we speak of a type of individual who is not socially well adjusted, we mean one who leads an unproductive life without any social interest. This is one way of classifying individuals, and perhaps it is the most important way. But consider the individual whose interest, however limited, is centered on visual things. Such a person differs entirely from one whose interests are largely concentrated on things oral, but both of them may have difficulty in social situations and find it difficult to establish contact with their fellow human beings. The classification by types can thus be a source of confusion if we do not realize that types are merely convenient abstractions.

Let us now consider the people who are to be our reference for measuring variations. They have a socially oriented life, and their way of life is such that, whether they intend it or not, society derives a certain advantage from their work. Also, from a psychological point of view they have enough energy and courage to meet life's problems and difficulties as they come along. Both of these qualities are missing in the case of psychopathic people: They are neither socially well adjusted nor are they psychologically adjusted to the daily tasks of life.

The "Maladjusted" Life Style

As an illustration of lack of adjustment we may take the case of a certain individual, a man of thirty who always escaped at the last moment from the solutions to his problems. He had a friend but was very suspicious of him, and as a result this friendship never prospered. Friendship cannot grow under such conditions, because the other person feels the tension in the relationship. This man really had no friends, despite the fact that he was on speaking terms with a large number of people. He was not sufficiently interested in other people to make friends. In fact he did not like being with people and was always silent in the company of others. He explained this by saying that in company he never had any ideas and therefore had nothing to say.

He was very shy. He had a pink skin and occasionally became flushed when he talked. When he could overcome this shyness he would speak quite well. What he really needed was to be helped in this direction without criticism. He was not very popular and he felt this, which increased his dislike for speaking to people. His life style was such that if he approached other people he only drew attention to himself.

Next to social life the most important question is the one of occupation. Our patient always had the fear that he might fail in his career, and so he studied day and night; he overworked himself. And because he suffered from the consequences of overwork, he put himself out of commission and became unable to meet the challenge of his occupation.

If we compare our patient's approach to these first two challenges in his life, we see that he always put himself under pressure. This is a sign that he had a great feeling of inferiority; he undervalued himself and looked on others and on new situations as being hostile to him. He acted as though he were in enemy territory.

We now have enough data to picture the life style of this man. We can see that he wants to go forward, but at the same time he is blocked because he fears defeat. It is as if he stands before an abyss, straining and always tense; he manages to go forward but only conditionally, and he prefers to stay at home and not deal with other people.

The third question with which this man was confronted—and it is a challenge for which most people are not very well prepared—is the challenge of love. He hesitated to approach women. He felt that he wanted to love and to be married, but because of his great feeling of inferiority he was too frightened to face the prospect. He could not accomplish what he wanted; we see his whole behavior and attitude summed up in the words, "Yes . . . but!" He fell in love with one woman after another. This is, of course, a frequent occurrence with neurotic people because in a sense two women are less than one; this truth shed some light on what lies behind a tendency toward polygamy or two-timing.

Let us discuss the reasons for this life style. Individual Psychology undertakes to analyze its causes. This man, like each one of us, established his life style during his first four or five years. At that time some tragedy must have happened that greatly influenced him, and so we must find out about this tragedy. Something made him lose his normal interest in others, and made him feel that it is better not to go on at all rather than to be always confronting difficult situations. He became cautious, hesitant, and a seeker of ways to escape.

He was the first child in the family. We have already discussed the great significance of this position; we have shown how the chief problem in the case of first children arises from the fact that they are for some time the center of attention, only to be displaced from their position of glory when another child comes along and appears to be preferred. In a great many cases where people are shy and afraid to go forward, we find the reason to be that they believe another person has been preferred. In this case it is not difficult to work out that this is where the trouble lies.

Methods of Diagnosis

Often we need only to ask a patient in our consulting room, "Are you the first, second, or third child in the family?" Then we have many of the clues we need. We can also use an entirely different method: We can ask for early memories, which we shall discuss at some length in the next chapter. This method is worthwhile because these memories or first pictures are a part of development of the early life style, which we have called the prototype. One comes upon an actual part of the prototype when people talk about their early memories. Looking back, everybody remembers certain important things, and indeed what remains preserved in somebody's memory is always important.

There are schools of psychology that act on the opposite assumption; they believe that what a person has forgotten is the most important. But there is really no great difference between these two ideas. Perhaps people can recount their conscious memories, but do not know what they mean—they do not see the connection with present actions. So the result is the same, whether we emphasize the hidden or forgotten significance of conscious memories or the importance of unconscious ones.

Descriptions of early memories are highly illuminating. A man might tell you that when he was small, his mother went shopping with him and his younger brother. He pictures himself and a younger brother. Therefore we immediately see it must have been important to him to have had a younger brother. Lead him further and you may find a situation similar to a certain case in which a man recalled that it began to rain while the family was out shopping. His mother took him in her arms, but when she looked at the younger brother she put him down so that she could carry the little one instead. Thus we can picture his life style: He always has the expectation that another person will be preferred. We can understand, therefore, why he cannot speak in the company of others, for he is always looking around to see if another will not push him out of the limelight. The same is true with friendship: He is always thinking that another will be preferred by his friend, and as a result he can never establish true friendship. He is constantly suspicious, looking out for little things that he can interpret as betrayal or rejection.

We can also see how the tragedy he has experienced has hindered the development of his social interest. He recalls that his mother took the younger brother in her arms, and we see that he feels that this baby had more of his mother's attention than he did. He is convinced that the younger brother is preferred and is constantly looking for confirmation of this idea. He is determined to be proved right, and so is always under strain—always under the great difficulty of trying to accomplish things when someone else is preferred.

The only solution apparent to such suspicious people is complete isolation, so that they will not have to compete at all with others and will be, so to speak, the only human beings on earth. Sometimes, indeed, such children will fantasize that the whole world suffered some disaster, that they are the only people left alive and hence no one else can have an advantage over them. We see how they tap all possibilities to comfort themselves, but they do not go along the lines of logic, common sense, or truth, rather along the lines of suspicion or private logic. They live in a private world and have a private idea of escape. They have absolutely no connection with others and no interest in others, but we can't blame them for we know that their mental processes are not "normal."

Developing Social Feeling

It is our task to help such people develop the social feeling demanded of a socially well-adjusted human being. How is this to be done? The great difficulty with individuals behaving this way is that they are overstrained and always looking for confirmation of their fixed ideas. It thus becomes impossible to change their ideas unless somehow we can penetrate their personality in a way that will question their preconceptions. To accomplish this, it is necessary to use both skill and tact. And it is best if the counselor is not closely related to or has an interest in the patient, for if one is directly concerned in the case, he will find that he is acting in his own interest and not in the interest of the patient. The patient will not fail to notice this and will become suspicious.

The important thing is to decrease patients' feelings of inferiority. They cannot be eliminated entirely, and in fact we do not want to do so because feelings of inferiority can serve as useful foundations on which to build. What we have to do is to change patients' goals. We have seen that their goal has been one of escape because someone else is preferred, and it is around this complex of ideas that we must work. We must decrease their feelings of inferiority by showing them that they really undervalue themselves. We can show them the mistakes in their actions and explain to them their tendency to be over-tense, as if they were standing before a great chasm or as if they were living in enemy territory, in constant danger. We can indicate to them how their fear that others may do better than them is standing in the way of them doing their best work and making the best impression.

If such people could act out the role of a host at a party, making sure their friends have a good time, being friendly with them, and thinking of their interests, they would improve tremendously. But in ordinary social life we see that they do not enjoy themselves, do not have constructive ideas, and as a result say, "Stupid people—they cannot enjoy being with me; they cannot interest me." The trouble with people suffering under these misconceptions is that they do not understand their situation because of their reliance on private logic and their lack of common sense.

Overcoming Depression and Fear

Let us now look at another specific case, the case of a man afflicted with depression. This is a very common illness, but it can be cured. People susceptible to depression can be identified very early in life. Many children, in their approach to new circumstances, show signs of suffering from depression.

The man in this case had about ten bouts of depression, and these always occurred when he started a new job. As long as he was in a familiar job he could be described as nearly "normal," but he did not want to go out, and he wanted to rule over others. Consequently, he had no friends, and at fifty he had never married.

Let us look at his childhood in order to study his life style. He had been very sensitive and quarrelsome, always dominating his older brothers and sisters by emphasizing his pains and his weaknesses. When playing on a couch one day when he was only four or five years old, he pushed all the other children off. When his aunt reproached him for this, he said, "Now my whole life is ruined because you have blamed me!"

Such was his life style—always trying to rule over others, always complaining of his weakness and of how much he suffered. This characteristic led to depression in his later life, which in itself is simply an expression of weakness. Many depressed patients use almost the same words: "My whole life is ruined. I have lost everything."[1] Frequently, such people have once been pampered and are so no longer, and this influences their life style.

For the most part, human beings have a tendency to be afraid. This timidity, when expressed in a social situation, is one of the most frequent causes of poor social adjustment. There was a man from an aristocratic family who never wanted to exert himself, but always wished to be supported and looked after. He appeared weak, and of

1. This again presents the question of nature versus nurture. Adlerians historically look at all behavior as goal directed or purposeful, but allowance has to be made for genetic predisposition and other biological factors.

course he could not find a job. His brothers turned against him, saying, "You are so stupid that you cannot even find a job. You don't understand anything." So he turned to drink. After some months, he was diagnosed as an alcoholic and was put in a treatment center for two years.

The treatment helped him but did not benefit him permanently, for he was sent back into the community without any preparation. He could find work only as a laborer, even though he was a scion of a well-known family. Soon he began to have hallucinations. He thought a man appeared before him to tease and torment him so that he could not work. First he could not work because he was an alcoholic, and then because he had hallucinations. And so we can see that it is not appropriate treatment merely to make alcoholics stop drinking; we must find and correct the errors in their life style. This man had been a pampered child, always wanting to be helped. He was not prepared to work alone.

We must help all children to become independent, and this can be done only if we get them to understand the mistakes in their life styles. In this case, the child should have been trained to do some useful work, and then he would not have had to be ashamed before his brothers and sisters.

V

CHILDHOOD MEMORIES

Discovering the Prototype

HAVING ANALYZED THE SIGNIFICANCE of an individual's life style, we turn now to the topic of childhood memories, which are perhaps the most important means for understanding a life style. By looking back through childhood memories we are able to uncover the prototype—the core of the life style—better than by any other method.

After we have heard a little about a patient's complaints, we ask her for her childhood memories and then compare them with the other facts she has given. For the most part, the life style never changes; there is always the same person with the same personality, a unity. A life style, as we have shown, builds up through the striving for a particular goal of superiority, and so we must expect every word, act, and feeling to be a part of this effort. At some points it is especially clearly expressed, and this happens particularly in childhood memories.

We should not, however, distinguish too sharply between early and recent memories, for in recent recollections too the pattern is involved. It is easier and more illuminating, however, to find the direction of striving at its beginning, for then we discover the basic theme and are able to understand that the life style of a person does not really change.

When patients look back into their past we can be sure that anything their memory turns up will be of emotional interest to them, and thus we will find a clue to their personality. It is not to be denied that forgotten experiences are also important for the life style and for the prototype, but often it is more difficult to have access to forgotten or, as they are called, unconscious memories. Both conscious and unconscious recollections have the quality of tending toward the same goal of superiority. They are both part of the complete prototype. It is advisable, therefore, to investigate both the conscious and unconscious memories if possible, because both are in the end equally important, and the individual herself generally understands neither. It is for the outsider to understand and interpret both.

Let us begin with conscious memories. Some people, when they are asked for early memories, answer, "I don't have any." We must ask such people to concentrate and try to remember. After some effort, we usually find that they will recall something. But this hesitation may be considered a sign that they do not want to look far back into their childhood, and we may then come to the conclusion that their childhood has not been pleasant. We have to encourage such people and give them hints in order to find out what we need to know. They invariably remember something in the end.

Some people, on the other hand, claim that they can remember back to when they were only one year old. This is scarcely possible, and the truth is probably that these are fancies and not true memories. But it does not matter whether they are imagined or true since either way they are parts of someone's personality.

Others insist that they are unsure whether they remember a thing or whether their parents later told them about it. This, too, is not really important because even if their parents did tell them, they have fixed the fact in their minds and therefore it helps to tell us where their interest lies.

Types of Memories

As we explained in the previous chapter, it is convenient for certain purposes to classify individuals into types. Childhood memories fall into types and reveal what is expected of the behavior of a particular type of person. For instance, let us take the case of a person who remembers that she saw a marvelous Christmas tree, filled with lights, presents, and baubles. What is the most interesting thing in this story? The fact that she saw these things. Why does she tell us what she has seen? Because she is always interested in visual things. She has perhaps struggled against some difficulties with eyesight, and having been trained, has always been more interested in and attentive to what she can see. Perhaps this is not the most important element of her life style, but it is an interesting and valuable part. It indicates that if we are to advise her on a suitable occupation it should be one in which she will use her eyes.

In school, the education of children often disregards this principle of types. We may find children interested in visual things who will not listen to the teacher because they always want to be looking at something. In the case of such children, we ought to be patient in trying to educate them to listen. Many children in school learn only in one way because they enjoy things with only one of their senses. They may be good only at listening or at seeing. Some always like to be on the move and working. We cannot expect the same results from different types of children, especially if the teacher prefers one teaching method, such as talking to the children. When such a method is predominant, the "lookers" and the "doers" will suffer and be hindered in their development.

Consider the case of a young man, twenty-four years old, who suffered from fainting spells. When asked for his childhood memories, he recalled that when he was four years old he fainted when he heard an engine whistle. In other words, he was a man who had heard, and was therefore interested in hearing. It is not necessary to explain here how this young man later developed fainting spells, but it is sufficient to note that from his childhood he was very sensitive to sound. He was very musical and could not bear unpleasant noises, disharmony, or strident tones. We are not surprised, therefore, that he should have been so affected by the sound of a whistle. Children or adults are often particularly interested in certain things because they have suffered through them. This was seen in the case of the man with asthma mentioned in chapter 2. His chest was bound tightly for some childhood complaint, and as a result he had developed an extraordinary interest in ways of breathing.

One meets people whose whole interest seems to lie in things to eat. Their childhood memories have to do with eating, and eating seems the most important thing in the world for them—how to eat, what to eat, and what not to eat. We will often find that difficulties connected with food or digestion in early life enhanced the importance of eating for such an individual.

A person may also have memories connected with movement and walking. Many children who could not move very well at the beginning of life because they were weak or suffered from enfeebling illnesses become abnormally interested in movement and always want to hurry. The following case serves as an illustration:

A man of fifty came to the doctor complaining that whenever he accompanied somebody across the road he suffered from a terrible fear that they would both be run over. When alone, he was never bothered with such a fear and was quite composed when crossing the road. It was only when someone else was with him that he felt compelled to save that person. He would grasp his companion's arm, push her to the right or to the left, and generally annoy her. Let us analyze the reasons for this behavior.

When asked for his childhood memories, he explained that when he was three years old he was physically weak and suffered from rickets. He was twice hit by vehicles while crossing a street. And so, now that he was a man, it was important for him to prove that he had overcome this weakness. He wanted to show, so to speak, that he was the only person who knew how to cross a street. He was always looking for an opportunity to prove it whenever he was with someone else. Of course, being able to cross a street safely is not something in which most people would take pride or want to compete with others. But with people like our patient, the desire to move nimbly and to show off the ability to do so can be quite strong.

Another case is that of a boy who was on his way to becoming a criminal. He stole, played truant from school, and so on, until his parents were in despair. His childhood memories revealed that he had always wanted to move around and to hurry. He was now working at his father's business and was sitting still all day. From the nature of the case, part of the treatment prescribed was that he be made a salesman—a traveler—for his father's business.

Death in the Family

One of the most significant types of childhood memories is the death of someone close during early childhood. When children see someone die, the effect on their minds is very marked. Sometimes such children become morbid; sometimes, without becoming morbid, they devote their whole lives to the problem of death and always struggle against illness and death in some way. We may find many of these children interested in medicine later in life, and they may become physicians or pharmacists. Such a goal, of course, is on the useful side of life. They not only engage in a private struggle against death, but they help others.

Sometimes, however, the prototype develops in an egotistical way. A child who was very much affected by the death of an older sister was asked what he wanted to be. The answer expected was that he would be a physician; instead, he replied, "A grave digger." When asked why he wanted to follow this occupation, he answered, "Because I want to be the one to bury the others and not the one who is buried." This goal, we see, is not constructive, for the boy is interested only in himself.

The Memories of Pampered Children

Let us turn now to consider the memories of those who were pampered as children. The early recollections mirror the characteristics of these people clearly. Children of this type often mention their mothers, which is perhaps natural, but can also be a sign that they have had to struggle for a favorable situation. Sometimes the memories seem quite innocuous, but they require careful analysis. For instance, a woman may tell you, "I was sitting in my room and my mother stood by the cabinet." This appears unimportant, but the mention of her mother is a sign that this has been a matter of interest to her. Sometimes the mother is more hidden and the study becomes more complicated; we have to guess about the mother. Thus the woman in question may tell you, "I remember making a journey." If you ask who accompanied her, you will discover it was her mother. Or, if children tell us, "I remember I was in the countryside one summer," we can guess that the mother was with the children, and see the hidden influence of the mother.

After studying many memories, we can see a struggle for preferment. We can see how a child in the course of her development begins to value the attention her mother gives her, and her memories concern the presence or absence of such attention. This is important for our understanding because if children or adults tell us about such memories, we may be sure that they always feel that they are in danger of losing something or that another will be preferred to them. We see a tension indicating that in later life such people will be of a jealous disposition.

Specific Memories

Sometimes people express interest in one point above all others. For instance, one patient's earliest memory was, "I had to watch my little sister one day, and I wanted to protect her as well as I could. I put her near the table but she caught the tablecloth and fell down." The child was only four years old at the time, which is of course an early age at which to permit a child to watch over a younger one. We can see what a tragedy this was in the life of the child, who was doing everything possible to protect the younger sister. This patient grew up and married a kind—we might almost say obedient—husband. But she was always jealous and critical, always afraid that her husband would prefer another. We can easily understand how the husband tired of her and concentrated on the children.

Sometimes tension is more directly expressed and people remember that they actually wanted to hurt other members of their family, even to kill them. Such people are interested in their own affairs exclusively and do not like other people—they feel a certain rivalry toward them. This feeling already is present in the prototype.

There are some people who can never finish anything because they fear someone else will be preferred as a friend or colleague, or because they suspect other people are always trying to surpass them. They can never really become a part of the community because of the fear that others might outshine them and be preferred. In every situation they are extremely tense, and this attitude is especially evident in connection with love and marriage.

We come now to the hated or unwanted child. This type, fortunately, is rare. If a child is really hated and neglected from the beginning of her life, she cannot live. Such a child will perish. Usually children have parents who pamper them to some extent and satisfy their desires, but we do find children who feel unwanted or hated, and we often see these children becoming depressed. Frequently we find in their memories an emphasis on being scolded, hated, or criticized.

A man came to a psychologist, for example, because he was always afraid to leave his home. His earliest memory was of running away because his mother constantly scolded and punished him, he then fell into a pond and almost drowned. We see from this memory that he left home once and met with great danger. Thereafter he constantly looked for danger when he went out. He had been a bright child but always feared that he might not gain first place in examinations, so he hesitated and could not go on. When he at last got to college he feared that he would not be able to compete with the other students. We see how all this may be traced back to his old memories of danger.

Another case that illustrates this is of an orphan whose parents died when he was only about a year old. He was not cared for properly in the orphanage. Nobody looked after him, and in later life it was very difficult for him to make friends or work with colleagues. Looking back to his early memories, we see that he always felt others were preferred. This feeling played an important part in his development: He always felt hated, and this hindered his approach to all life's problems. He was excluded from all the normal situations of life, such as love, marriage, friendship, work—all the situations that required contact with his fellow human beings—because of his feeling of inferiority.

A further interesting case is that of a middle-aged man who was always complaining of sleeplessness. He was about forty-six, married, and had had children. He was very critical of everybody and was always trying to act the tyrant, particularly over members of his family. His behavior made everyone feel miserable.

When asked for his childhood memories, he explained that he had grown up in a home with quarrelsome parents, who were always fighting and threatening each other, so that he was afraid of them both. He went to school dirty and uncared for. One day his usual teacher was absent and a substitute took her place. This woman was interested in her job and saw that it was good and noble work. She saw possibilities in this unkempt boy and went out of her way to encourage him. This was the first time in his life he had any such treatment. From that time on he began to develop well, but it was always as if he were pushed from behind. He did not really believe he was able to do well, and so he worked all day and half the night too. In this way he grew up believing that he must use half the night for his work, or else not sleep at all but spend the time thinking about what he had to do. He believed it was necessary to be awake almost all night to accomplish anything worthwhile.

Later, his desire to be superior was expressed in his attitude toward his family and in his behavior toward others. His family, being weaker than he was, allowed him to play the role of a conqueror with them. Inevitably his wife and children suffered much through this behavior.

Summing up the character of this man as a whole, we may say that he had a goal of superiority and that it was the goal of a person with a great feeling of inferiority. His tenseness was a sign of his doubt of his own success, and this doubt in turn was covered up by a pose of superiority. A study of childhood memories can thus be shown to reveal the situation in its true light.

Predictive Analysis

If we can analyze childhood memories, we can predict, as we have said, what will happen later in the life of our patients. Memories are signs of what happened in a person's life and how development took place; they indicate the movement toward a goal and what obstacles have had to be overcome. They also show how people become more interested in one side of life than another. We see that they may have suffered a trauma in a sexual matter, for instance; therefore, they may be more interested in such matters than in others. We cannot be surprised if, when we ask for early memories, we hear of some sexual experiences. Sex interests some people more than others at an early age. Naturally, it is part of normal human behavior to be interested in sex, but, as I have said before, there are many varieties and degrees of interest. We often find that in a case where people tell us about sexual experiences, they later put emphasis on this aspect of life. The resulting life style is not harmonious because this one side of human nature is overvalued. There are people who insist that every experience has a sexual basis. On the other hand, there are those who insist that the stomach is the most important part of the body, and we will find that early memories also parallel later preoccupations in such instances.

There was a boy who would never settle down at high school. He wanted to be constantly moving and would never concentrate on studying. He was always thinking about something else, frequenting cafes and visiting friends—all when he should have been studying. It was therefore interesting to examine his early memories.

"I can remember lying in my cot and looking at the wall," he said. "I noticed the paper on the wall, with all its flowers and patterns." This boy was prepared only for lying in a cot, not for studying or taking examinations. He could not concentrate on his studies because he was always thinking of other things and daydreaming. We can see that he was a pampered child and could not work alone.

Even if we cannot completely cure such people we can help them, with the skillful study of childhood memories, to understand and improve their situation.

VI

EXPRESSIONS OF THE LIFE STYLE

In the last chapter we tried to describe the way in which childhood memories and fancies may be used to illuminate the hidden life style of an individual. The study of childhood memories is only one method of studying personality. All methods depend on the principle of using isolated parts for an interpretation of the whole. Besides childhood memories, we can also observe characteristic physical movements and mental attitudes. Bodily postures and movements are an expression of psychological attitudes, and these attitudes are an expression of that whole approach to life that constitutes what we call the life style.

Body Language

Let us first discuss bodily movements. We unconsciously judge people by their manner of standing, walking, and sitting, their facial expressions, and so on. We do not always consciously judge, but these impressions usually create a basic feeling of sympathy or antipathy.

Let us consider ways of standing, for instance. We notice straight away whether a child or adult stands upright or hunched and bent over. But we have to watch for exaggerations, such as people who stand too straight, in a stretched position; this makes us suspect that they are using too much effort to retain this posture. We can suppose that these people feel much smaller than they want to appear. In this minor point we can see how they mirror what we call the superiority complex. They want to appear courageous.

On the other hand we see people with just the opposite posture: those who appear bent and are always stooping. Such a posture suggests that they are cowards. But it is a rule of our art and science that we should always be cautious, looking for other points and never judging solely by one criterion. Sometimes we might feel that we are almost sure of being correct, but we still want to verify our judgment by weighing up other points. We might ask, "Are we right in insisting that people who stoop are often cowards? What can we expect of them in a difficult situation?"

Such people often try to rest upon something, to lean on a table or chair, for instance. They do not trust their own strength and want to be supported. This reflects the same attitude of mind as that characteristic of people who stand bent over, and so when we find both types of posture present, it reinforces our judgment to a certain extent.

Children who always want support and protection do not have the same posture as independent-minded children. We can tell the degree of independence by how children stand, and how they approach other people. In such cases we need not have any doubt, for there are many ways of confirming our conclusions. And once we have confirmed them, we can take steps to remedy the situation and put the child on the right path.

Thus we may experiment with children who constantly seek support. Sit their mother on a chair and then let the children come into the room. We will find that they do not look at any other person but go directly toward their mother and lean on the chair or against their mother. This confirms what we expect: Children feel dependent.

It is also interesting to note children's ways of approaching others, for this shows the degree of social interest and social adjustment. It expresses the confidence, or lack of confidence, that children have in others. We will find that people who do not want to approach others and who always stand far away are also reserved in other respects; they may rarely speak and are usually quiet.

As an illustration, let us take the case of a woman who came to a doctor for treatment. The doctor expected her to take a seat near him, but when he offered her a chair she looked around and took a seat some distance away. It could only be concluded that this was a person who wanted to connect only with certain people. She said straight away that she was married, and from this the whole story could be guessed: She wanted to be connected only with her husband. It could also be guessed that she wanted to be pampered, that if she was alone she would suffer great anxiety, that she would never want to go out of her house alone and would not enjoy meeting other people. In short, from her one physical movement we could arrive at a good guess about the whole story. But there are other ways of confirming our theory.

She may tell us, "I am suffering from anxiety." We know that anxiety can be used as a weapon with which to rule another person. If adults or children suffer from anxiety, we can guess that there is another person in their lives who supports them.

There was once a couple who insisted that they were free thinkers. Such people believe that everybody can do what he or she wants in a marriage, as long as each one tells the other what happens. Consequently the husband had some love affairs and told his wife all about them. She seemed perfectly content, but later on she began to suffer from anxiety. She would not go out alone. Her husband always had to go with her. We can see then how she used her anxiety or phobia to modify this aspect of their relationship.

Timidity

Let us analyze the prototype of a timid and hesitating person. There was a boy who came to school seeming very shy. This is an important sign that he did not want to be connected with others. He had no friends and was always anxiously waiting for the time when he could go home. He moved very slowly and would go down the school steps keeping to the wall, then look down the street and rush toward his house. He was not a good pupil at school and did poorly in his work, since he did not feel happy inside the school walls. He always wanted to go home to his mother, a widow who was weak and pampered him very much. To understand more about the case, the doctor talked with the mother.

He asked her, "Does the boy want to go to bed at bedtime?" She replied that he did.

"Does he cry out at night?"

"No."

"Does he wet the bed?"

"No."

The doctor thought that there must be some mistake. Then he realized what the reason was: The boy must sleep in the same bed as his mother. How did the doctor reach this conclusion? Well, to cry out at night would be to demand the mother's attention. If the boy was sleeping in her bed, this would not be necessary. Similarly, to wet the bed is also to demand the mother's attention. The doctor's conclusion was verified: The boy slept in his mother's bed.

If we look carefully, we will see that all the little things to which the psychologist pays attention form part of a consistent plan of life. Hence when we can see the goal—in this child's case, to be always close to his mother—we can conclude a great many things. We can conclude by this means whether a child is lacking in intelligence. An unintelligent child would not be able to establish such a clever plan for life.

Moods

Let us turn to the mental attitudes we can distinguish in different people. Some people are quarrelsome and aggressive, others seem ready to give up the struggle. However, we never see a person who really gives up. This is not possible, for it is beyond human nature: The "normal" person cannot give up. If a person seems to do so, it indicates an even more desperate struggle to carry on than otherwise.

There is a type of child who always seems to give up. Such children are usually the center of attention in a family, and everybody has to care for them, push them forward, and admonish them. They must be supported in life and are always a burden to others. This is their goal of superiority: They express their desire to dominate others in this fashion. Such a goal of superiority is, of course, the result of an inferiority complex, as we have already shown, for if they were not doubtful of their own powers, they would not take this easy way of attaining success.

There was a boy of seventeen who illustrated this characteristic. He was the oldest in his family. We have already seen how the oldest child often experiences a tragedy when the coming of another child dethrones him from his place at the center of family affections. This was the case with the boy. He was very depressed and peevish, and he had no job. One day he tried to commit suicide. Soon after that he visited a doctor and explained that he had had a dream before his suicide attempt. He dreamed he had shot his father. We see how such a person—depressed and inert—has at all times the possibility of dramatic action present in his mind. We also see how children who are lazy at school, and indolent adults who seem incapable of doing anything, may be on the brink of danger. Often this indolence is only on the surface. When something happens, they may attempt suicide or other violence, or develop a neurotic condition or mental disturbance. To ascertain the mental attitude of such people is sometimes a difficult scientific task.

Shyness in a child is another characteristic that is full of danger. Shy children must be treated carefully. Such children will always have great difficulties unless their shyness is overcome, for in our culture only courageous and outward-looking people achieve good results and benefit from the advantages of life. If people are courageous and suffer defeat they are not hurt so much, but shy people tend to make their escape to the useless side of life as soon as they see difficulties ahead. Such children may become neurotic or even insane in later life.[1]

1. There are shy children who, as adults, may become more socially reserved. What is most telling in how a shy child will develop is how that child is treated by a parent: with encouragement or with pampering or overprotection.

We see such people going about with shamefaced expressions, and when they are with others they hesitate and do not speak, or they avoid people altogether.

The Development of Personal Characteristics

The characteristics we have been describing are mental attitudes. They are not inborn or inherited, but are simply reactions to a circumstance. Any given characteristic of mine is the answer that my life style gives to my perception of a problem that confronts me. Of course it is not always the logical answer that a philosopher would expect. It is the answer that my childhood experiences and mistaken perceptions have trained to give me.

We can see how these attitudes function as well as how they have developed more clearly in children or in "abnormal" people than "normal" adults. The life style is portrayed more clearly and simply in the prototype stage than in later stages. In fact, one may compare the functioning of the prototype to that of a tree, which assimilates everything that comes along—manure, water, food, air—in its development. The difference between the prototype and the later stages of the life style is like the difference between a tree with unripe fruit and a tree with ripe fruit. The unripe fruit stage in human beings is much easier to open up and examine, but what it reveals is to a significant extent valid for the ripe fruit stage.

We can see, for example, how children who are cowardly at the beginning of life express this cowardice in all their attitudes. A world of differences separates cowardly children from aggressive ones. Aggressive children always have a certain degree of courage, a natural outgrowth of what we have called common sense. Sometimes, however, very cowardly children may appear heroic in certain situations; this happens whenever they are deliberately trying to attain first place.

The case of the boy who could not swim illustrates this clearly. One day he went into the water with other boys who had asked him to join them. The water was very deep, and the boy nearly drowned. This, of course, is not real courage and could be described as being on the "useless" side of life. The boy merely did what he did because he wanted admiration. He ignored the danger he was in and hoped that others would save him.

Masters of Our Own Fate

The question of courage and timidity is psychologically closely related to the belief in predestination. The belief in predestination affects our capacity for useful action. There are people who have such a feeling of superiority that they feel they can accomplish anything; they believe they know everything and do not want to learn anything new. We have seen the result of such ideas. Children who feel this way in school usually get poor marks. There are other people who want to participate in the most dangerous sports—they feel that nothing can happen to them, that they cannot suffer defeat. Very often the outcome is a bad one.

We commonly find this sense of privileged destiny among people to whom something terrible has happened, yet who have remained unhurt. For example, they may have been involved in a serious accident and escaped uninjured. As a result they feel that they are destined for higher things.

There was once a patient who had such a feeling, but after going through an experience whose outcome differed from his expectation he lost courage and became depressed. His most important support had fallen away. When asked for his childhood memories, he related a significant experience.

He was once about to go to a theater in Vienna but had to attend to something first. By the time he finally arrived at the theater, it had burned down. Everything was destroyed, but he had been saved. We can understand how he felt himself privileged and destined for higher things. He believed in his invincibility until his relationship with his wife failed, and then he broke down.

Much could be said and written about the significance of such a belief in fatalism. It affects whole peoples and civilizations, let alone individuals, but I wish to point out only its connection with the sources of psychological activity and the life style. The belief in predestination is in many ways an escape from the task of striving and working on a useful activity. For that reason, it will prove a false support.

Envy and Jealousy

One of the basic mental attitudes that most affects our relations with our fellow human beings is that of envy. To be envious is a sign of feeling inferior. We all have a certain amount of envy in our makeup, and a small amount does no harm. We must, however, ensure that envy serves a useful purpose. It must result in work, in perseverance, and in facing our problems. If it does, we should excuse the bit of envy found in each of us.

On the other hand, sexual jealousy—a situation in which a person fears losing a partner to another—is a much more difficult and dangerous mental attitude, because it cannot be made useful. There is no single way in which a jealous person can be useful. Moreover, we see in jealousy the fruit of a deep feeling of inferiority. A jealous person is afraid of his inability to keep his partner. And so at the very moment when one partner wishes to influence the other most, he betrays his weakness by expressions of jealousy. If we look at the prototype of such a person we shall see a sense of defeat; that person is probably someone who has been dethroned and expects to be dethroned again.

The Masculine Protest

From the general problem of envy and jealousy we may pass to the consideration of a particular type of envy: the envy of the female sex for the social position of the male sex. We find many women and girls who want the privileges of being male, and thus take on male qualities and attitudes to achieve them. This attitude, which I have termed the "masculine protest," is quite understandable. If we look at society impartially, we can see that in our culture men are all too often in the lead—more appreciated, valued, and esteemed than women. Morally, this is inexcusable and ought to be corrected.

Girls see that in the family, the men and boys are privileged and less burdened with the smaller cares of life, which are left to the women. Men are freer in many ways, and this perceived freedom makes girls dissatisfied with their role. Therefore they try to act like boys. This imitation of boys may appear in various ways: We see them, for instance, trying to dress like boys, and their parents support this. But some actions are potentially destructive, such as when a girl insists on being called by a boy's name and not her own. Such girls get very angry if others do not call them by the name they have chosen. This attitude is dangerous if it reflects something profound and is not a mere prank. In such a case, it may reappear later in life as a dissatisfaction with the feminine role and a distaste for the sexual role of a woman.

It is appropriate for women to develop like men in many ways and to have professions commonly held by men, but it is dangerous for them to be dissatisfied with their feminine role and try to adopt the vices of men.

This dangerous tendency first makes its appearance in adolescence, for it is then that the prototype becomes affected. Immature girls may become jealous of the privileges enjoyed by the boys. They react with the desire to imitate boys. This is a superiority complex and a departure from proper development.

Anyone who believes that the basis of relationships between the sexes should be the principle of equality should not encourage this masculine protest on the part of women. The equality of the sexes can fit into the natural scheme of things, while the masculine protest is a blind revolt against reality and is thus a superiority complex. Through this masculine protest, all the sexual functions can be disturbed. Many serious symptoms can be produced, and if we trace them back we shall see that the condition started in childhood.

Not so frequently as in the case of girls who want to be boys, we also encounter boys who wish to be like girls. They want to imitate not the ordinary girls, but those who flirt in an exaggerated manner. Such boys may use face powder, wear flowers, and act frivolously. This is also a form of superiority complex.

We find, in fact, that in many cases such boys grew up in environments in which a woman was at the head of the family. Thus the boys grew up imitating the characteristics of the mother, not of the father.

There was a boy who came for consultation because of certain sexual problems. He related how he was always close to his mother, and his father did not have a significant role in the home. His mother had been a dressmaker before she married and continued her occupation afterward. The boy, being always near her, became interested in the things she made. He began to sew and draw pictures of dresses for women. The extent of his interest in his mother can be judged from the fact that at four years of age he had learned to tell the time because his mother always went out at four o'clock and came back at five. Impelled by his pleasure on seeing her return, he learned to tell the time.

Later in life, when he went to school, he acted like a girl. He took no part in sports or games, and the other boys made fun of him. One day they had to put on a play, and as we may imagine, this boy had the part of a girl. He acted it so well that many in the audience thought he really was a girl. In this way, the boy came to believe that he could not be much appreciated as a man, but he could be greatly appreciated as a woman. This was the genesis of his later sexual problems.

VII

DREAMS

The Life of Dreams

For Individual Psychology, consciousness and unconsciousness form a single entity, as we have already explained in a number of contexts. In the last two chapters, we have been interpreting elements of consciousness—memories, attitudes, and physical movements—in terms of the individual whole. We shall now apply the same method of interpretation to our unconscious or semiconscious life—the life of dreams. The justification for this method is that our dream life is just as much a part of the whole as our waking life. Followers of other schools of psychology are constantly trying to find new approaches to dreams, but our understanding of dreams developed along the same line as our understanding of all the integral parts of the psyche.

Just as our waking life is dominated by the goal of superiority as we have seen, our dreams are also determined by our individual goals. A dream is always a part of the life style, and we always find the prototype involved in it. In fact, it is only when you see how the prototype is connected with a particular dream that you can be sure you have really understood the dream. Also, if you know people well, you can pretty nearly guess the nature of their dreams.

Take, for instance, our assumption that humankind as a whole is not courageous. From this general fact we can presuppose that a large proportion of dreams will be dreams of fear, danger, or anxiety. And so, if we know someone well and see that her goal is to escape from having to solve life's problems, we can guess that she often dreams about falling down. Such a dream is like a warning to her: "Do not go on—you will be defeated." She expresses her view of her future in this way—by falling. The majority of people have similar dreams of falling at some time in their lives.

A specific case is a student on the eve of an examination—a student whom we know to be lacking in determination. We can guess what will happen with her. She worries the whole day preceding the examination, cannot concentrate, and finally says to herself, "There is not enough time." She wants to postpone the examination. Her dream will be one of falling down, and this expresses her life style.

Take another student who makes good progress in her studies, is courageous, and never uses subterfuges. We can also guess her dreams. Before an examination, she will dream that she climbs a high mountain, is enchanted with the view from the mountain top, and then awakens. This is an expression of the current of her life, and we can see how it reflects her goal of accomplishment.

Then there are people who limit their potential—people who can proceed only up to a certain point. Such people dream about limits and about being unable to escape from people or difficulties. They often have dreams of being chased and hunted.

Before we go on to discuss the purpose of dreams, it may be well to remark that the psychologist is never discouraged if somebody says, "I cannot tell you any dreams because I never remember them. But I will make up some dreams." The psychologist knows that people's imagination cannot create anything other than that which their life style commands. Their made-up dreams are just as good as genuinely remembered dreams, for their imagination and fancy will also be an expression of their life style.

Fancy need not literally reflect people's real actions to be an expression of their life style. We find, for example, one type of person who lives more in imagination than in reality. They are cowardly during the day but quite courageous in dreams. In them, we will find an indication that they do not want to finish any real work. Such manifestations will be quite evident even in their most courageous dreams.

The Purpose of Dreams

The purpose of a dream is to pave the way toward the goal of superiority; that is, the individual's private goal of superiority. All of a person's characteristics, actions, and dreams are tools to enable him or her to find this dominating goal—whether it is one of being the center of attention, of domineering, or of escape.

The purpose of a dream is neither logically nor truthfully expressed within it. A dream exists to create a certain feeling, mood, or emotion, and it is impossible to unravel its obscurities fully. But in this, it differs from waking life and the activities of waking life only in extent, not in character. We have seen that the answers the psyche gives to life's problems are relative to the individual's scheme of life: They do not fit into a pre-established frame of logic, although it is our aim, for the purposes of improved social communications, to make them do so more and more. Once we relate it firmly to waking life, dream life loses its mystery. It becomes a further expression of the same attitudes, and the same mixture of fact and emotion that we find in waking life.

Historically, dreams have seemed very mysterious, with many cultures giving them prophetic interpretations. Dreams were often regarded as prophecies of events to come, and in this there was a half-truth. It is true that a dream is a bridge connecting the problem confronting dreamers with the goals they wish to attain. In this way dreams will often come true, because dreamers will be training for their part during the dream, and will be thus preparing for it to come true.

Similarly, there is the same interconnectedness revealed in dreams as in our waking life. If people are perceptive and intelligent they can foresee the future whether they analyze their waking life or their dream life. What they do is diagnose. For example, if somebody dreams that an acquaintance has died and the person does actually die, this might be no more than what a doctor or close relative could foresee. What the dreamer does is to think in his sleep rather than in waking life.

The prophetic view of dreams, precisely because it contains a certain half-truth, is a superstition. It is generally clung to by people who are superstitious by nature, or promoted by people who see importance by giving the impression that they have special powers.

To dispel the prophetic superstition and the mystery that surrounds dreams, we have to explain why most people do not understand their dreams. The explanation is found in the fact that few people know themselves even in waking life. Few people have the power of reflective self-analysis that permits them to see where they are headed, and the analysis of dreams is, as we have said, a more complicated and obscure affair than the analysis of waking behavior. It is thus no wonder that the analysis of dreams should be beyond the scope of most people, and it is also no wonder that in their ignorance of what is involved they should turn to charlatans.

Dream Logic

It will help us to understand the logic of the dream if we compare it, not directly with normal waking life, but with the type of phenomena we have described in previous chapters as manifestations of private logic. The reader will remember how we described the attitudes of criminals, problem children, and neurotics: They create a certain feeling, temper, or mood to convince themselves of a certain fact. Thus murderers may justify themselves by saying, "Life has no use for this person; therefore we must kill him." By emphasizing in their minds the view that their victims are unwanted, they create a certain feeling that prepares them for murder.

Such people may also reason that so-and-so has a nice car and they do not. They put such value on this that they become envious. Their goal of superiority becomes that of having a nice car, and so we may find them experiencing dreams that create a certain emotion leading to the accomplishment of that goal. We see this illustrated, in fact, in well-known dreams. There are, for instance, the dreams of Joseph in the Bible. In one, he dreamed that all his brothers bent down before him. Now we can see how this dream fits in with the whole episode of the coat of many colors—and with Joseph's banishment by his brothers.

Another well-known dream is that of the Greek poet Simonides, who was invited to go to Asia Minor to lecture. He hesitated and continually postponed the trip in spite of the fact that his ship was in the harbor waiting for him. His friends tried to make him go, but to no avail. Then he had a dream. He dreamed that a dead man whose body he had found and for whom he had arranged burial appeared to him and said, "Because you cared enough to give me a decent burial, I now warn you not to go to Asia Minor."

Simonides said, "I will not go," and the ship on which he was to have sailed was lost with all aboard. He believed the dream had saved him, but he had already been inclined not to go before he ever had the dream. He simply created a certain feeling or emotion to back up a conclusion that he had already reached, although he did not understand his dream.

It is clear that one can create a fantasy for the purposes of self-deception, which results in a desired feeling or emotion. Frequently this feeling is all one remembers of the dream. In considering Simonides's dream we come to another point: What should be the procedure in interpreting dreams? First, we must bear in mind that a dream is part of a person's creative power. Simonides, dreaming, used his fancy and built up a story. He selected the incident of a dead man. Why should this poet pick the incident of the dead man from out of all his other experiences? Obviously, he was very much concerned with ideas of death at the time, because he was terrified at the thought of sailing on a ship. In those days a sea voyage presented real danger, and so he hesitated. It is a sign that he was probably not only afraid of seasickness, but also that he feared the ship would sink. As a result of this preoccupation with the thought of death, his dream selected the episode of the dead man.

If we consider dreams in this manner, the task of interpretation is not too difficult. We should remember that the selection of images, memories, and fancies is an indication of the direction in which the mind is moving. It shows you the dreamer's tendency, and ultimately we can see the goal she is striving for.

Let us consider, for example, the dream of a certain married man who was not content with his family life. He had two children but he always worried about them, thinking that his wife did not take sufficient care of them and was too interested in other things. He always criticized his wife and tried to reform her. One night he dreamed that he had a third child and this child was lost and could not be found. In the dream he reproached his wife because she had not taken care of the child.

Here we see that he had in mind the thought that one of his two children might be lost, but he was not courageous enough to make one of them the victim in his dream. So he invented a third child and made him get lost.

Another point to be observed is that the man loved his children and did not want to lose them. Also, he felt that his wife was overburdened with two children and could not care for three, and so this third child would perish. Hence we find another aspect to the dream, which, when interpreted, reads: "Should I have a third child or not?"

The result of the dream was that he created a bad feeling against his wife. No child was really lost, but he got up in the morning criticizing her and feeling antagonistic toward her. People frequently get up in the morning feeling argumentative and critical as a result of an emotion created by that night's dream. It is like a state of intoxication and not unlike what one finds in depression, where patients intoxicate themselves with the ideas of defeat, of death, and of all being lost.

We may also see that this man selected situations in which he was sure to be superior, as revealed by his feeling, "I am careful with the children, but my wife is not and therefore one got lost." Thus the dream reveals his tendency to dominate.

Methods of Interpretation

Modern interpretation of dreams dates from the early part of the twentieth century. Dreams were first regarded by Freud as the fulfillment of infantile desires. I cannot agree with this; if dreams are such a fulfillment, then everything can be regarded as a fulfillment. Every idea behaves in this way, going from the depths of the subconscious up into consciousness. The formula of sex-fulfillment thus explains nothing in particular.

Later Freud suggested that the desire for death was involved. But surely our last example could not be explained very well in these terms, for we cannot say that the father *wanted* a child to get lost and die, or to die himself.

The truth is that there is no specific formula with which to explain all dreams, except the general principles we have discussed about the unity of mental life and about the special emotional character of dream life. This character, and its accompanying self-deception, is a theme with many variations. It is also expressed in a preoccupation with comparisons and metaphors. The use of comparisons is one of the best means of deceiving oneself and others, for we may be sure that if people use them they do not feel sure that they can convince others with facts and logic. They always want to influence others by means of useless and far-fetched comparisons.

Poets use these devices to deceive, but pleasantly, and we enjoy being entertained by their metaphors and poetic comparisons. We may be sure, however, that they are meant to influence us more than we would be influenced by plainer words. If Homer, for example, speaks of an army of Greek soldiers overrunning a field like lions, the metaphor will not deceive us when we think rationally, but it will certainly intoxicate us when we are taken by the poetic mood. The author makes us believe in a marvelous power, but he could not do this if he were merely to describe the clothes the soldiers wore, the arms they carried, and so on.

We see the same thing in the case of people who have difficulty explaining something: If they see they cannot convince you, they will use comparisons. This use of metaphors and comparisons, as we have said, is self-deceptive, and this is the reason it is so prominent in dreams in the selection of symbolic images. It is an artistic way of intoxicating oneself.

Dreamers and Nondreamers

The fact that dreams are emotionally intoxicating offers, curiously enough, a method for *preventing* dreams. If people understand what they have been dreaming about and realize that they have merely been intoxicating themselves, they will stop dreaming. To dream will have no more purpose for them. At least, this is the case with me; I stopped dreaming as soon as I realized what dreaming meant.

This realization, to be effective, must be a thorough emotional conversion. This was brought about, in my case, by my last dream. The dream occurred during the First World War. In connection with my duties I was making a great effort to keep a certain man from being sent to the front. In the dream the idea came to me that I had murdered someone, but I did not know whom. I got myself into a bad state wondering, "Whom have I murdered?" The fact is that I was simply intoxicated with the idea of making the greatest possible effort to keep the soldier in a safe place. The dream emotion was meant to be conducive to this idea, but when I understood the subterfuge of the dream, I gave up dreaming altogether, since I did not want to deceive myself in order to do the things that, for reasons of logic, I should either do or leave undone.

This may be taken as an answer to the question that is frequently asked, "Why do some people never dream?" These are people who do not want to deceive themselves. They are concerned with action and logic and want to face problems. People of this sort, if they dream, often forget their dreams quickly, so quickly in fact that they believe they have not been dreaming.

There is a theory that we always dream but forget most of our dreams. If we accepted such a theory it would shed a different light on the fact that some of us never dream; we would become people who always forget their dreams. I do not accept this theory. I rather believe that there are people who never dream, and there are also dreamers who sometimes forget their dreams. In the nature of the case such a theory is hard to refute, but perhaps the burden of proof should be put on the propounders of the theory.

Why do we sometimes have the same dream repeatedly? This is a curious fact for which no definite explanation can be given. However, in such repeated dreams we are often able to find our life style expressed with greater clarity. Such a repeated dream gives us a definite and unmistakable indication as to where our individual goal of superiority lies. In the case of long, extended dreams, we must believe that the dreamers are not ready and are looking for the way out from their problem to the achievement of their goal. For this reason, the dreams that can best be understood are short dreams. Sometimes a dream consists of only one image, or a few words, and it shows that dreamers are really trying to find an easy way to deceive themselves.

Sleep and Hypnotism

We may close our discussion with the question of sleep. A great many people ask themselves needless questions about sleep. They imagine that sleep is the direct opposite of being awake, and that it is akin to death. But such views are erroneous. Sleep is not the opposite of being awake, but rather a degree of wakefulness. We are not cut off from life during sleep. On the contrary, we think and hear in our sleep, and the same tendencies are generally expressed in sleep as in waking life. Thus, there are mothers who cannot be awakened by any noises in the street, but if the children make the slightest sound they immediately jump up. We see from this how their interest is always awake. Also, from the fact that we do not fall out of bed we can see that we are conscious of limits during sleep.

An individual's entire personality is expressed when she is both asleep and awake. This explains the phenomenon of hypnotism. What charlatans have represented as a magical power is for the most part nothing more than a kind of sleep. But it is a sleep during which people want to obey another and know that the hypnotist wants to make them sleep. A simple form of the same thing is when parents say, "That's enough—now go to sleep!" and the children obey. Hypnotism, too, works because the subjects are obedient. The ease with which individuals may be hypnotized is in proportion to their obedience.

In hypnotism we have an opportunity to make people imagine scenes, ideas, or memories that their waking inhibitions block. The only requirement is obedience. By this method we can often discover forgotten early memories.

As a method of treatment and cure, however, hypnotism has its dangers. I do not like hypnotism and use it only when a patient responds to no other method. One will find that hypnotized people can be rather vengeful. In the beginning they appear to overcome their difficulties, but they do not really change their life style. Hypnotism is like a drug or a mechanical aid: The individual's true nature has not been touched. What we have to do is to give people courage, self-confidence, and better understanding of their mistakes if we are really to help. Hypnotism does not do this and should not be used except in rare cases.

VIII
PROBLEM CHILDREN

Principles of Education

How SHALL WE EDUCATE our children? This is perhaps the most important question in our present social life, and it is a question to which Individual Psychology has a great deal to contribute. Education, whether carried on in the home or at school, is an attempt to bring out and direct the personalities of individuals. The science of psychology is thus a necessary basis for proper educational technique; we may look upon all education as a branch of that vast psychological art of living.

Let us begin with certain preliminaries. The most general principle of education is that it must be consistent with the later life that individuals will be called upon to face. This means that it must be consistent with the ideals of the nation. If we do not educate children in society's ideals, then these children are likely to encounter difficulties later in life. They will not fit in as members of society.

The ideals of a nation may change. They may change suddenly, such as after a revolution, or gradually, in a process of evolution. But this simply means that the educator should keep in mind a broad ideal. It should be an ideal that will always have its place and will teach individuals to adjust themselves properly to changing circumstances.

The connection of education with social ideals is influenced by its connection with the rule of government, and it is in the government's interest that national ideals should be reflected in the school system; the government cannot readily reach the parents or the family, but it monitors what is happening in the schools.

Historically, schools have reflected different ideals at different periods. In Europe, schools were originally established for aristocratic families and were aristocratic in spirit. Later on, the church took over the schools, and only priests were teachers. Then, as the nation's demands for more knowledge began to increase, more subjects were taught and a greater number of teachers was needed than the church could supply. So others besides priests and clergy entered the teaching profession.

Until quite modern times teachers were rarely exclusively teachers but followed another trade, such as shoemaking, tailoring, and so on. Many of them knew how to teach only by using the rod. Their schools were not the sort of places in which children's psychological problems could be solved.

The beginning of the modern spirit of education came in Europe in Johann Heinrich Pestalozzi's time. Pestalozzi was a Swiss educational reformer and the first teacher to promote methods other than the rod and punishment. He showed the great importance of proper methods in schools. Today, with correct methods, every child—unless he has learning difficulties—can learn to read, write, sing, and do arithmetic. We cannot say that we have already discovered the best methods; they are in the process of development all the time. As is right and proper, we are always searching for new and better methods.

Formerly in Europe, only aristocrats were influential, and there was a demand only for officials on the one hand and for laborers on the other. Those who had to prepare for a higher station went to school; the rest had no education at all. The educational system reflected the ideals of the time. Today, in Europe as well as the United States, the school system responds to a different set of national ideals. We no longer have schools in which children must sit quietly, hands folded in their laps, and not move. Now we have schools in which the children are the teacher's friends. They are no longer compelled by authority merely to obey, but are encouraged to develop more independently and to think for themselves.

The connection between the school system and national and social ideals is organic, because of its origin and organization, as we have seen. From a psychological point of view, the connection with social ideals gives schools a great advantage as educational agencies. The principal aim of education is social adjustment. The school can guide the current of sociability in the individual child more easily than the family because it is much nearer to the needs of the nation and less susceptible to the children's demands and criticism. It does not pamper the children and in general has a much more detached attitude.

The family, on the other hand, is not always permeated with social ideals. Too often we find traditional disciplinarian ideas or sheer materialism dominating there. Only when the parents are themselves socially well adjusted and understand that the aim of education must be social can progress be made. Wherever parents know and understand these things, we will find children properly prepared for school, just as in school they properly prepare for their special place in life. This should be the ideal development of the child at home and in school, with the school standing midway between the family and the nation.

Understanding Parents and Children

In previous chapters we have noted that the life style of a child is fixed after he is four or five years old and cannot be directly changed. This indicates the way in which the modern school must progress. It must not criticize or punish, but try to mold, educate, and develop the social interest of children. The modern school cannot work on the principle of suppression and punishment, but rather on the idea of trying to understand and solve children's personal problems.

On the other hand, since parents and children are so closely united in the family, it is often difficult for parents to educate their children for society. They prefer to educate them for their own aspirations and thereby create a tendency that will cause conflict for their children in later life. Such children are bound to face great difficulties and are already confronted with problems the moment they enter school.

To remedy this situation it is necessary to educate parents. Often this is not easy, for we don't have access to the elder members of the family as we do to the children. And even when we reach the parents, we may find that they are not much interested in the ideals of society. They are so concerned with their own problems that they do not want to understand.

Not being able to do much with the parents, we simply have to content ourselves with spreading more understanding as best we can. The best point of attack is in schools, first because large numbers of children gather there; second, because mistakes in the life style appear more clearly there than in the family; and third, because teachers are trained to understand children's problems.

The Superiority Complex in Problem Children

"Normal" children, if there be such a category, do not concern us. If we see children who are fully developed and well adjusted socially, the best thing is not to stand in their way. Such children can be depended upon to look for a useful goal in which to develop their sense of superiority. Their superiority feeling, precisely because it is on the useful side of life, is not a superiority complex.

On the other hand, problem children—neurotics, delinquents, and so on—express a superiority complex as a compensation for their feelings of inferiority. These feelings of inferiority, as we have shown, exist in all human beings, but only become a complex when they discourage people to the point of driving them to destructive or useless behavior.

All these problems of inferiority and superiority have their root in family life during the period before children enter school. It is during this period that they have built up their life style, which is in contrast to the adult life style we have designated as a prototype.[1] This prototype is the unripe fruit, and like all unripe fruit, if there is a worm in it, the more it develops and ripens, the larger the worm grows.

1. Adler initially referred to the formative years, from infancy to age five or six, as the prototype for the ultimate personality or life style. After these formative years, the life style is pretty much in place and unlikely to change unless psychotherapy is engaged. Adler subsequently ceased using the term *prototype.*

As we have seen, the difficulty often develops from physical problems or organ inferiority. It is not the organic inferiority that causes the problem but the social maladjustment it brings in its wake. It is here that the educational opportunity lies, because if we can train people to adjust themselves socially, the organic problems may become assets. For as we have seen, a physical problem may spark a striking interest, developed through training, which may rule the individual's whole life. Provided this interest runs in a useful channel, it may be advantageous.

It all depends on how the organic difficulty fits in with social adjustment. Thus in the case of children who are interested only in seeing or only in hearing, it is up to the teacher to develop their interest in the use of all their senses. Otherwise, they will be at a disadvantage compared with other pupils.

In addition to the attention children with imperfect organs require, a problem is presented by the great number of pampered children who come to school. With the way schools are organized, it is impossible for a single child always to remain the center of attention. Occasionally a teacher may be so kind and soft-hearted that he panders to favorites, but as such children move from class to class, they fall out of their position of favor. Later in life it is even worse, for it is not considered proper for one person always to be the center of attention without doing anything to merit it.

All such problem children have certain defined characteristics. They are not well equipped to meet the problems of life; they are ambitious and want to achieve success individually, not on behalf of society. In addition, they are often quarrelsome and at loggerheads with others. They are usually cowards, since they lack interest in all the problems of life.

Some Characteristics of Problem Children

Other characteristics we often discover among such children are that they are cautious and continually hesitating. They postpone solving the problems that life poses, or else they come to a stop altogether when faced with problems, going off on a tangent and never finishing anything.

These characteristics come to light more clearly in school than in the family. School is like an experiment or acid test, for there it becomes obvious whether a child adjusts to society and its problems. A mistaken life style often passes unrecognized at home, but it becomes all too readily apparent in school.

Both the pampered child and the child with physical problems always want to escape the difficulties of life because of their great feeling of inferiority, which robs them of the strength to cope. However, we may control their difficulties at school and thus gradually put them in a position to solve problems. The school thus becomes a place where we really educate and not merely give instruction.

We see, then, that whether or not teachers and officials like it, an understanding of all these problems and of the best methods for handling them must be developed as part of the school curriculum.

Gifted Children

Besides these problem children, there are also children who are believed to be prodigies—the exceptionally bright children. Sometimes, because they are ahead in some subjects, it is easy for them to appear brilliant in others. They are sensitive, ambitious, and not usually very well liked by their comrades. Children immediately seem to feel whether one of their number is socially well adjusted or not. Such prodigies are admired but not highly regarded.

We can understand how many of these gifted children pass through school satisfactorily. But when they enter social life they have no adequate plan of life. When they approach the three great problems of life—society, employment, and relationships—their difficulties appear. What happened in their prototype years becomes apparent, and we see the effect of their not being well adjusted in the family. There they continually found themselves in favorable situations, which did not bring out the mistakes in their life style. But the moment a new situation comes their way, the mistakes appear.

The solution that Individual Psychology offers for the problems of prodigies is the same as that for other children. The Individual psychologist says, "Everybody can accomplish everything." This is a democratic maxim that takes the pressure off prodigies, who are always burdened with expectations, are always pushed forward, and become too much interested in themselves. People who adopt this maxim can have very brilliant children who do not become conceited or too ambitious. They understand that what they have accomplished was the result of training and good fortune. If their good training continues, they can accomplish much. But other children, who are less well favored and not as well trained and educated, may also accomplish good things if their teacher can encourage them.

How to Encourage Children

These latter children may have lost courage, and must therefore be protected against their marked feeling of inferiority, a feeling that none of us can suffer for long. One can understand their being overwhelmed by difficulties at school and, as a result, misbehaving or else not going to school at all. They believe that there is no hope for them at school, and if this were true we should have to agree that they are acting consistently and rationally. But Individual Psychology does not accept the belief that their case is hopeless at school; it believes that everybody can accomplish useful work. There are always mistakes, but these can be corrected and the child can go on.

Often, however, the situation is not handled well. At the very time when the child is overwhelmed by new difficulties at school, parents adopt a watching and anxious attitude. Any bad school reports, criticisms, or scoldings that the child gets at school are magnified by repercussions at home. Often children who behave well at home, because they have been pampered, become badly behaved in school because their latent inferiority complex shows up the moment they lose contact with the family and are no longer the center of attention. It is then that such children will hate the pampering parent because they feel deceived. The parent does not appear in the same light as he did before. All the old pampering is forgotten in the anxiety of the situation.

We often find children who are aggressive at home are quiet, calm, and even inhibited at school. Sometimes a parent comes to school and says, "This child takes up all my time and attention. He is always fighting."

The teacher replies, "He sits quietly all day at school and does not move." This is simply the reverse of the former situation; the child receives attention at school and for that reason is quiet and unassuming. At home he is not the center of attention, and so he fights.

There is the case, for example, of an eight-year-old girl, who was very well liked by her schoolmates and was at the top of her class. Her father came to the doctor saying, "This child is very sadistic—a real tyrant. We can no longer bear her." What was the reason? She was the first child in a weak family. Only a weak family could be so intimidated by a child. When another child was born, this girl felt herself in danger, and still wanting to be the center of attention as before, she began to be aggressive. At school she was liked and appreciated, and, not having any reason to fight, she developed well.

Some children have difficulty both at home and in school. Both family and teachers complain, and the result is that the children's mistakes increase. Some are chronically untidy at home and in school. Now if the behavior is the same both within the family and at school, we must look for the cause in things that have gone before. In any case we must always consider behavior both in the family and in school in order to form a judgment on children's problems. Every part of their lives becomes important for us if we are correctly to understand their life style and the direction in which they are striving.

It sometimes happens that fairly socially well-adjusted children, when faced with the new situation school presents, may seem unable to cope. This usually happens when children come to a school where the teacher and other pupils are hostile. For example, if children who are not from the upper classes are sent to an aristocratic school, they may suffer because they are regarded as not having the "right" background, and their colleagues will seem to be against them. Such children, who may previously have been pampered, or at least cosseted, suddenly find themselves in a very hostile atmosphere; sometimes the cruelty of other children can be astonishing. In many cases, children who experience this never speak a word about it at home because they feel ashamed. They suffer their terrible ordeal in silence.

Often such children, when they come to the age of sixteen or eighteen—the age at which they have to behave like adults and face life's problems squarely—stop short because they have lost courage and hope. And along with their social difficulties comes problems in relationships, because they cannot find their place in society.

What are we to do with such cases? They have no outlet for their energies. They are separated, or feel separated, from the whole world. The type of people who want to hurt themselves for the sake of hurting others may commit suicide. On the other hand, there are also types who want to disappear, and they isolate themselves, losing even the few social abilities they once had. They do not speak to people in the ordinary way, do not approach people, and are always antagonistic toward the world. This state, when acute, we call *schizophrenia.* If we are to help any of these people we must find a way to rebuild their courage. They are very difficult cases, but they can be cured.

Inasmuch as the treatment and cure of children's educational problems depend primarily on the diagnosis of their life styles, it is appropriate to review here the methods that Individual Psychology has developed for this diagnosis. The diagnosis of the life style is of course useful for many other things besides education, but it is quite essential in educational practice.

Besides conducting a direct study of children during their formative years, Individual Psychology methods involve asking children for early memories and for their plans concerning a future occupation, observing posture and movement, and making certain inferences from the child's place in the family. We have discussed all these methods before, but it is perhaps necessary to emphasize again the position of the child in the family, as this is the most closely connected with educational development.

Birth Order and Family Dynamics

The important thing about the order of children in the family is, as we have seen, that a first child is temporarily in the position of an only child and is later dethroned from that position. He or she thus enjoys great power for a while, only to lose it. The psychology of the other children is fixed and determined by the fact that they are not first children.

Among oldest children we often find that a conservative view prevails. They have the feeling that those in power should remain in power; it is only an accident that they have lost their own power, and they have great admiration for powerful people.

Second children are in an entirely different situation. They go through life, not as the center of attention, but with a pacemaker running ahead of them. They always want to catch up. They do not recognize the sanctity of authority, but think it should change hands. They feel an impulse to go forward urgently, as in a race. All their movements show that they are fixing their attention on a point ahead to catch up with it. They are always trying to change the laws of science and nature, and are really revolutionary—not so much politically, but in social life and in their attitude toward their fellow human beings. We have a good example of this in the biblical story of Jacob and Esau.

The position of the youngest in the family is of remarkable interest from a psychological point of view. By youngest we mean of course children who will always be the youngest and will never have any successors. Such children are in an advantageous position since they can never be dethroned. Second children may be dethroned, and sometimes they experience the same tragedy as first children, but this can never happen in the lives of youngest children. They are therefore the most favorably situated, and other circumstances being equal, we find that these children show the best development. They resemble second children in that they are energetic and try to overcome others; they too, have pacemakers. But in general they take an entirely different path from the rest of the family. If the family includes several scientists, the youngest will probably work in the arts or commerce. If the family runs a business, the youngest may become a poet. Youngest children must always be different. For it is easier to work in another area than to have to compete in the same field of employment, and for that reason youngest children like to follow a different line from the rest. This is also a sign that they are somewhat lacking in courage, for were such children courageous, they would be more willing to compete in the same field.

Note that our predictions of character based on the position of children in the family are merely tendencies; there is no certainty about them. And in fact if a first child is bright, that child may not at all be conquered by the second, and thus will not suffer any tragedy. Such children adjust well socially, and their parents are likely to have encouraged their interest toward others, including the newborn baby. On the other hand, if a first child cannot be conquered, this poses a greater problem for the second, and this second child may experience difficulties. Such second children often lose courage and hope. We know that children competing in a race must always have the hope of winning; when this hope is gone, all is lost.

Where there are several children who are nearly grown up before another is born, the last child finds himself in a situation similar to that of an only child. Only children also have their tragedy, for they have been the center of attention in the family throughout their childhood, and their goal in life is always to be at the center. They do not reason along logical lines, but along the lines of their own life style.

The position of an only boy among a family of girls is also difficult. It is commonly supposed that such a boy will behave in a girlish manner, but this view is rather exaggerated. After all, most of us are educated and cared for predominantly by women. However, there is a certain amount of difficulty when a boy grows up surrounded only by females. He may strive to appear more of a man and exaggerate this feature of his character, or he may indeed grow feminine like the rest of the household. In short, we will usually find that such a boy is either soft and mild or else very aggressive. In the latter case it would seem that he is always trying to prove and emphasize the fact that he is a man.

The only girl among boys is in an equally difficult situation. Either she is very quiet and develops strong femininity, or she wants to do everything that the boys do and will behave like them. A feeling of inferiority is quite apparent in such a case, since she is the only girl in a situation where boys are felt to be superior. The inferiority complex lies in the feeling that she is only a girl. In this word only the whole inferiority complex is expressed. We see the development of a compensating superiority complex when she tries to dress like the boys and when, later in life, she wants to have the kind of sexual relations that she understands men have. Again, we see the masculine protest present.

We may conclude our discussion of the position and gender of children in a family with the particular case where the first child is a boy and the second a girl. Here there is usually fierce competition between the two. The girl is pushed forward not only because she is the second child but also because she is a girl. She makes more effort and thus shows markedly the characteristics of a second child. She is energetic and independent, and the boy notices how she always seems to be gaining on him in the race. As we know, it is a fact that girls at first develop more rapidly both physically and mentally than boys. A girl of twelve, for instance, is much more mature than a boy of the same age. The boy sees this and cannot explain it. Hence, he feels inferior and has a longing to give up. He does not progress and starts looking for ways of escape. Sometimes he develops a constructive way of escape, and in other cases he may become neurotic, criminal, or insane. He does not feel strong enough to carry on with the race.

This type of situation is a difficult one to solve even with the attitude that "Everybody can accomplish everything." The main thing we can do is to show the boy that if the girl seems to be ahead it is only because she makes more effort, and by working harder he can find better methods of development. We can also seek to direct the girl and the boy into noncompetitive fields, as far as possible, so as to diminish the impression that they are running a race.

IX

SOCIAL ADJUSTMENT

The Social Context

THE GOAL OF INDIVIDUAL PSYCHOLOGY is *social* adjustment. This may seem a paradox, but if it is a paradox, it is only a verbal one. The fact is that it is only when we pay attention to the concrete psychological life of the individual that we come to realize how all-important the social element is. The individual becomes an individual only in a social context. Other systems of psychology make a distinction between what they call individual psychology and social psychology, but for us there is no such distinction. Our discussions hitherto have attempted to analyze the individual life style, but the analysis has always been from a social point of view and has had a social application.

We will now continue our analysis with more emphasis on the problems of social adjustment. The principles to be discussed are the same, but instead of concentrating our attention on diagnosing life styles, we shall discuss life styles in action and the methods for furthering proper action.

The analysis of social problems builds directly on our analysis of educational problems, the theme of the previous chapter. The school and nursery are miniature social institutions, and we can study there the problems of social maladjustment in a simplified form.

Behavioral Problems

Take the behavioral problems of a boy of five. His mother came to the doctor complaining that her son was restless, hyperactive, and troublesome. She was always at full stretch trying to control him, and at the end of the day she was exhausted. She said she could not cope with the boy anymore and was willing to have him taken into care if such action was advisable.

From these details we can readily identify with the boy. We can easily put ourselves in his place. If we hear that a child of five is hyperactive, we have no difficulty imagining what his behavior is like: He would climb over the furniture and would often get into trouble. If his mother wanted to read, he would play with the lights, or if his mother and father wanted to talk or listen to music he would yell. He would have temper tantrums if he did not get what he wanted, and he would always want something.

If we note such behavior in a young boy, we may be sure that he wants to fight and that everything he does is designed to provoke a fight. He is restless day and night, while his father and mother are always tired. The boy is never tired because unlike his parents he does not have to do anything against his will. He simply wants to be restless and keep others occupied.

A particular incident well illustrates how this particular boy fought to be the center of attention. One day he attended a concert at which his mother and father played the piano and sang. In the middle of a song the boy called out, "Hello Daddy!" and ran all around the hall. One could have predicted this, but the mother and father did not understand the reason for such behavior. They treated him as a normal child, in spite of the fact that he did not behave normally.

To this extent he was, however, normal: He had an intelligent life plan. What he did was cleverly done, in accordance with his plan. And if we see the plan we can guess the actions that would result from it. Hence we may conclude that the boy is not lacking in intelligence.

When his mother had visitors, he would push them off their chairs and always wanted the particular chair upon which someone was about to sit. We see how this, too, is consistent with his goal and with his prototype. His goal is to be superior and to rule others and always occupy the attention of his father and mother.

We can judge that he used to be a pampered child, and that were he to be pampered again, he would not fight. In other words, he was a child who had lost his favored position.

How did he lose it? The answer is, he must have acquired a younger brother or sister. He is thus a five-year-old in a new situation, dethroned and fighting to regain his important central position, which he believes he has lost. For that reason he always keeps his father and mother busy. But there is another reason. One can see that the boy has not been prepared for the new situation and that in his life as a pampered child, he did not develop any social feeling. He is thus not socially well adjusted. He is interested only in himself and occupied only with his own welfare.

When his mother was asked how her son behaved toward his younger brother, she insisted that he liked him, but that whenever he played with him he always accidentally pushed him over. We might be pardoned for assuming that such actions do not indicate marked affection.

To fully understand the significance of this behavior, we should compare it to the cases we frequently meet of aggressive children who do not fight all the time. The children are too intelligent to fight continuously, for they know that the father and mother would put an end to their fighting. Hence such children from time to time stop their fighting and put on their best behavior. But the old impulse reappears, as it does in this case when, in the course of playing with his younger brother, the boy pushes him over. His goal in playing is, in fact, to push the child over.

Now what is the boy's behavior toward his mother? If she tries to spank him, he either laughs and insists that the spank does not hurt him, or if she hits him a little harder, he becomes quiet for a while, only to begin his fighting again a little later. One should notice how all the boy's behavior is conditioned by his goal and how everything he does is without exception directed toward it, to the extent that we can predict his actions. We could not predict them if the prototype were not a unity, or if we did not know the goal of the prototype's impulses.

Imagine this boy starting out in life. He goes to nursery school, and we can predict what will happen there. In general he will rule in a weak environment, or in a more difficult one, he will fight in an attempt to rule. And so his stay at nursery school is likely to be short if the teacher is severe. In that case the boy might try to find subterfuges and would be constantly under tension; this tension might make him suffer headaches, restlessness, and so on. The symptoms would appear as the first signs of a neurosis.

On the other hand, if the environment were easy and pleasant, he might feel that he was the center of attention. Under such circumstances, he might even be at the top of the class.

Nursery school, as we can see, is a social institution with social problems. Individuals must be prepared for such problems because they have to follow the laws of the community. Children must be able to make themselves useful to that little community, and they cannot be useful unless they are more interested in others than in themselves.

In later years of school, the same situation would be repeated, and we can imagine what would happen to problem children of this sort. Things might be a little easier if they attended a private school, as these often have fewer pupils to whom more attention can be paid. Perhaps in such an environment problem children could be less noticeable. Teachers might even find them to be their best pupils. It is also possible that if a child like this were at the top of the class, his or her behavior at home might change—he or she might be satisfied to be superior in this way only.

Adjusting to School

In cases where children's behavior improves after they go to school, one may take it for granted that they have a favorable situation in their class and feel superior there. Usually, however, the opposite is true. Children who are very much loved and very obedient at home often disrupt the class at school.

In the last chapter we discussed the school as standing midway between the home and life in society. If we apply that formula, we can understand what happens to such children when they go out into life. Life will not offer them the favorable situation they may sometimes find in school. People are often surprised and cannot understand how children who are well behaved at home and successful at school should have problems in later life. We are here dealing with problem adults who have a neurosis that may later become serious. No one understands such cases because the prototype has been concealed by favorable situations until adult life.

We must learn, therefore, to recognize the mistaken prototype in a favorable situation, or at least to realize that it may exist, since it is very difficult to understand it in such circumstances. There are a few signs that may be taken as definite indications of a mistaken prototype. Children who want to attract attention and who lack in social interest often are untidy. By being untidy, they occupy other people's time. They also don't want to go to sleep and cry out at night or wet the bed. They play at anxiety because they have noticed that anxiety is a weapon by which they may force others to obey them. All these signs appear even in favorable situations, and by looking for them one is likely to spot any problems.

Facing the Three Tasks of Life

Let us consider a boy with such a mistaken prototype later in life, when he is on the verge of maturity, say at seventeen or eighteen. There is a great *hinterland* of life behind him, a hinterland that is not easily evaluated because it is not very distinct. It is not easy to see his goal and his life style. But as he faces life, he has to meet what I have called the three great tasks of life—the tasks of building successful human relationships, of pursuing a socially useful occupation, and of developing intimate relationships. These tasks arise out of the social relationships bound up in our very existence; the first involves our behavior toward other people, our attitude toward humankind and its future. This involves the preservation and the salvation of our species, for human life is so precarious that we can survive only if we pull together.

Regarding occupation in this case, we can judge from what we have seen of the boy's behavior at school that if he seeks an occupation with the idea of being superior, he will have difficulty in obtaining it. It is difficult to find a position where one will not sometimes be subordinate, or where one will not have to work with others. But as this boy is interested only in his own welfare, he will never get along well in a subordinate position, and moreover, such a person does not prove trustworthy in business. He can never subordinate his own interests to the interests of the firm.

In general we may say that success in an occupation is dependent on effective social adjustment. It is a great advantage in business to be able to understand the needs of colleagues and customers, to see with their eyes, hear with their ears, and feel as they feel. Such empathetic people will get ahead, but the boy we are studying cannot do so, for he always looks out solely for his own interests. He can do only a part of what is necessary for progress. Hence he will often be a failure in his occupation.

In most cases, one finds that such people never complete their training for an occupation, or at least, are late in taking up a career. They may be thirty years old and still do not know what they intend to do in life. They frequently change from one course of study to another, or from one type of job to another.

Sometimes we find girls or boys of seventeen or eighteen who are striving, but do not know what direction to take. It is important to be able to understand such people and to advise them regarding the choice of a vocation. They can still become interested in something, study it from the beginning, and train properly. But it is rather disturbing to find people of this age not knowing what they want to do in later life. They are too often the type who do not accomplish much.

Both at home and at school, efforts ought to be made to interest children in their future occupations long before they reach this age. In school and college this might be achieved by having discussion groups or giving assignments on possible career options.

The last question that young people have to face is that of love, marriage, and intimate relationships in general. Inasmuch as human beings are living as two sexes, this is an all-important question. It would be very different if there were only one gender. As it is, we have to learn ways of behaving toward the other sex. We shall discuss the question of love and marriage at length in a later chapter; here it is only necessary to show the connection between personal relationships and the problems of social adjustment. The same lack of social interest that is responsible for social and occupational maladjustment is also responsible for the common inability to form good relationships with the other sex. A person who is exclusively self-centered does not have the proper preparation for being half of a couple. Indeed it would seem that one of the chief purposes of the sexual instinct is to pull individuals out of their shells and prepare them for social life. But psychologically we have to meet the sexual instinct halfway—it cannot accomplish its function properly unless we are already predisposed to forget our own selves and merge into a larger life.

The Need to Build Character

We may now draw some conclusions about this boy we have been studying. We have seen him stand before the three great tasks of life, despairing and afraid of defeat. We have seen him with his personal goal of superiority excluding as far as possible all the questions of life. What then is left for him? He will not join in society, he is antagonistic to others, he is suspicious and reclusive. And being no longer interested in others, he does not care how he appears to them, and so he will often be untidy and dirty. Language, we know, is a social necessity, but our subject does not wish to use it. He does not speak at all—a trait seen in schizophrenia.

Blocked by a self-imposed barrier against all the questions of life, our subject is heading straight to the mental hospital. His goal of superiority brings about isolation from others, and it perverts his sex drives. We find him sometimes thinking he is Jesus Christ or the president of the United States. Only in this way can he manage to express his goal of superiority.

As we have frequently said, all the problems of life are, at bottom, social problems. We see social problems expressed in the nursery, in school, in friendships, in politics, in economic life, and so on. It is evident that all our abilities are socially focused and designed for the use of humankind.

We know that a deficiency in social adjustment begins in the prototype; the question is how to correct this before it is too late. If the parents could be told not only how to prevent the large mistakes but also how to recognize the small ones in the prototype and how to correct them, it would be a great advantage. But the truth is that it is not possible to accomplish much in this way. Few parents are inclined to learn and to avoid mistakes. They are not interested in questions of psychology and education, and either pamper their children and are antagonistic to anyone who does not regard them as perfect jewels, or else they are not sufficiently interested. Usually, not much can be accomplished through them; it is impossible to give them a good understanding in a short enough time. It would take a great deal of time to teach parents and advise them of what they should know. It is much better, therefore, to call in a doctor or psychologist.

Outside the work of the doctor and psychologist, the best results can be accomplished only through schools and education. Mistakes in the prototype often do not appear until a child enters school, and teachers familiar with the methods of Individual Psychology will soon notice a mistaken prototype. Teachers can see which children join the others, which children want to be the center of attention by pushing themselves forward, and which children lack courage. Well-trained teachers could recognize the mistakes of a prototype in the first week of exposure to a child.

Teachers, by the very nature of their social function, are well equipped to correct the mistakes of children. Schools were started because the family was not able to educate children adequately for the social demands of life; the school is the extension of the family, and it is there that children's characters form to a great extent and where they are taught to face the problems of life.

All that is necessary is that schools and teachers be equipped with the psychological insight that will enable them to perform their tasks properly. In the future, schools will surely make more use of the discoveries of Individual Psychology, for the true purpose of a school is to build character.

X

SOCIAL FEELING AND COMMON SENSE

Social Usefulness

We have seen that social maladjustment is caused by the social consequences of the sense of inferiority and the striving for superiority. The terms *inferiority complex* and *superiority complex* describe the state of affairs after a maladjustment has taken hold. These complexes are not in the genes nor in the bloodstream; they simply happen in the course of the interaction between individuals and their social environment.

Why don't such complexes happen to all individuals? All individuals have a sense of inferiority, and a striving for success and superiority makes up the very life of the psyche. The reason all individuals do not have complexes is that their feelings of inferiority and superiority are harnessed by a psychological mechanism into socially constructive channels. The springs of this mechanism are social feeling, courage, and the logic of common sense.

Let us study both the functioning and nonfunctioning of this mechanism. As long as the feeling of inferiority is not too great, we know that children will always strive to do something worthwhile and to work on the useful side of life. Such children, in order to gain their ends, are interested in others. Social feeling and social adjustment are the right and normal compensations, and in a sense it is almost impossible to find anybody—child or adult—in whom the striving for superiority has not resulted in such development. We can never find anyone who could say truly, "I am not interested in others." They may act this way—as if they were not interested in the world—but they cannot justify themselves. They claim, on the contrary, to be interested in others, in order to hide their lack of social adjustment. This is mute testimony to the universality of social feeling.

Hidden Complexes

Nonetheless, maladjustment does take place. We can study their genesis by considering marginal cases—cases in which an inferiority complex exists but is not openly expressed because conditions are favorable. The complex is then hidden, or at least there is a tendency to hide it. If people are not confronted with a difficulty, they may seem wholly contented. But if we look closely, we shall see how they really express—if not in words, at least in attitudes—the fact that they feel inferior. This is an inferiority complex, and people who are suffering from such a complex are always looking for relief from the burdens they have imposed upon themselves through their self-centeredness.

It is interesting to observe how some people hide their inferiority complex, while others confess in so many words, "I am suffering from an inferiority complex." The confessors are always elated at their confession and feel better than others because they have confessed while others have not. They say to themselves, "I am honest. I do not lie about the cause of my suffering." But at the same time as they confess their inferiority complex, they hint at difficulties in their lives or other circumstances that are responsible for their situation. They may speak of their parents or family, of not being well educated, or of some incident or restriction they suffered.

Often the inferiority complex may be hidden by a superiority complex, which acts as compensation. Such people are arrogant, impertinent, conceited, and snobbish. They lay more weight on appearances than actions.

In the early strivings of a person of this type, one may find a certain nervousness, which is thereafter used to excuse all the person's failures. He or she says, "If I did not suffer from bad nerves, what could I not do!" These sentences, with *if*, generally hide an inferiority complex.

An inferiority complex may also be indicated by such characteristics as slyness, cautiousness, pedantry, the exclusion of the larger problems of life, and the search for a narrow field of action limited by many principles and rules. It is also a sign of an inferiority complex if people always lean on something, even if they do not need to. Such people do not trust themselves, and we will find that they develop unusual interests and occupy themselves with little things, such as collecting trivia. People waste their time in this way and always find an excuse for themselves. They train themselves too much toward useless things, and this training, when prolonged, leads to a compulsion neurosis.

Symptoms of Neurosis

An inferiority complex is unusually hidden in all problem children no matter what type of problem they present on the surface. Thus, to be lazy is in reality to exclude the important tasks of life and is a sign of a complex. To steal is to take advantage of another; to lie is not to have the courage to tell the truth. All these manifestations in children have an inferiority complex at their core.

A neurosis is a well-developed form of inferiority complex. What can people not accomplish when they are suffering from an anxiety neurosis! They may be constantly wanting to have someone accompany them; if so, they succeed in their purpose. They are supported by others and force others to be occupied with them. Here we see the transition from an inferiority to a superiority complex. Other people must serve! In getting other people to serve them, neurotics become superior.

In all such cases where complexes develop, failure to function in social and useful channels is due to a lack of courage. It is this lack of courage that prevents individuals from following a social course. Side by side with lack of courage are the intellectual accompaniments of a failure to understand the necessity and utility of social life.

All this is most clearly illustrated in the behavior of criminals, who embody cases of inferiority complexes *par excellence.* Criminals are cowardly and stupid; their cowardice and social stupidity go together as two sides of the same coin.

Heavy drinking may be analyzed on similar lines. Alcoholics seek relief from their problems, and, instead of going through the work to solve them, are cowardly enough to be satisfied with the relief that comes from the bottle.

The ideology and intellectual outlook of such people differ sharply from the social common sense that accompanies a normal, courageous attitude. Criminals, for instance, always make excuses for themselves or accuse others. They mention the impossibility of finding a job, they speak of the cruelty of society in not supporting them, or they say that deprivation drove them on. When sentenced, they often use excuses like that of a child murderer who said, "It was done by a command above." Another murderer, upon being sentenced, said, "'What is the use of a boy like the one I killed? There are a million other boys." Then there is the "philosopher," who claims that it is not wrong to kill a mean old woman with a lot of money, when so many worthy people are starving.

The logic of such arguments strikes us as frail. The whole outlook of such people is conditioned by a socially useless goal, just as the selection of that goal is conditioned by a lack of courage. Criminals always have to justify themselves, whereas a goal on the useful side of life speaks for itself and does not need any excuses.

A Case History

Let us examine an actual clinical case that illustrates how social attitudes and goals can transform into antisocial ones. Our case involves a girl who was nearly fourteen. She grew up in a good home where the father, a hardworking man, had supported the family as long as he was able to work, but his health had failed. The mother was a kind and honest woman and was very much interested in her six children. The first child was a very intelligent girl who died at the age of twelve. The second girl was ill but later recovered and took a job to help support the family. The next child was the subject of our case history. This girl was always healthy, and since her mother had always been occupied with the two sick girls and with her husband, she did not have much time for this girl, whom we shall call Anne. There was a younger boy who was also highly intelligent, but who suffered from poor health, and as a result Anne found herself crushed, so to speak, between two very much loved children. She was a good child, but she felt that she was not as well liked as the others and complained of being slighted and of feeling that she was held back.

In school, however, Anne worked hard and was at the top of her class. But when she was thirteen and a half and went on to high school, she had a new teacher who did not like her. Perhaps she made a bad start; whatever the reason, lack of appreciation made her worse.

She was not a problem child as long as she was appreciated by her old teacher; she had had good reports and was well liked by her schoolmates. But an Individual psychologist could have seen even then that something was wrong by looking at her friendships. She always criticized her friends and tried to dominate them. She wanted to be the center of attention and to be flattered, but never to be criticized herself.

Anne's goal was to be appreciated, favored, and protected. She found she could accomplish this only in school, not at home. When she changed schools she found appreciation blocked there, too; the teacher scolded her, told her she was badly prepared for lessons, and gave her bad reports. Finally she became a truant and stayed away altogether for several days. When she came back, the situation was worse than ever, and in the end the teacher proposed that she be expelled from the school.

Expulsion from school accomplishes nothing. It is a confession on the part of the school and the teachers that they cannot solve a particular problem. But if they cannot solve the problem, they should call in others who perhaps might be able to help. After talking with Anne's parents, arrangements might have been made to try another school, or another teacher might have gotten along better with Anne. But her teacher did not reason that way; she reasoned, "If a child plays truant and does bad work, she must be expelled." Such reasoning is a manifestation of private logic, not of common sense, and common sense is especially vital in a teacher.

We can guess what happened next. The girl lost her last hold on life and felt that everything was falling apart for her. After being expelled from school, she lost even the slight amount of appreciation she had at home, so she ran away from both home and school. She disappeared for many days and nights, and finally it was discovered that she had had a love affair with a soldier.

We can understand why; her goal was to be appreciated, and up to this time she had tried to do useful work, but now she turned away from it. The soldier appreciated her and liked her at first. Later, however, the family received letters from her saying that she was pregnant and that she wanted to kill herself.

This action of writing to her parents was in line with her character—she was always turning in the direction in which she expected to find appreciation, and eventually turned back to her home. She knew that her mother would be in despair about her and that she would not, therefore, be scolded. Her family, she felt, would be only too glad to take her in again.

In treating a case of this sort, the skill of identification—the ability to place oneself sympathetically in the situation of the person involved—is all-important. Here is someone who desperately wants to be appreciated and is pushing toward this one goal. We should identify ourselves with such people and ask, "What would I do in that situation?" It is also important to try to encourage such people, but always toward useful activities. We should try to get them to the point where they say, "'Perhaps I need a change of school, but I am not stupid. Perhaps I have not tried hard enough; perhaps I have not paid enough attention; perhaps I tried to do things in my own way too much at school and did not understand the teacher." If it is possible to give a person courage, then he will learn to make this effort on the useful side of life. It is lack of courage compounded by an inferiority complex that causes problems.

Another person of the same age and in the same position as Anne might turn to crime. Such cases are quite common: If children lose courage at school, they may drift into criminal activity or become a member of a violent group. Such behavior is easily understood. When children lose hope and courage, they begin to play truant, fabricate excuses, not do their homework, and look for places to spend their days away from school. In such places they find companions who have followed the same path before them and whom they join. They lose all interest in school and withdraw more and more into a private world.

Providing Encouragement

The inferiority complex is often connected with the idea that a person has no special abilities. It is a commonly held fallacy that some people are gifted and others are not. Such a view is itself an expression of an inferiority complex. According to Individual Psychology, everybody can accomplish everything, and it is a sign of an inferiority complex when a boy or girl despairs of following this maxim and feels unable to accomplish a useful goal.

Another aspect of the inferiority complex is the belief in inherited characteristics. If it were entirely true that success were dependent upon innate ability, then no psychologist could help anyone. But in reality success is largely dependent on courage, and the task of the psychologist is to transform feelings of despair into feelings of hopefulness, which rally a person's energies for useful effort.

Sometimes we encounter cases of young people of sixteen or so who are expelled from school and commit suicide out of despair. The suicide is a sort of revenge—an accusation against society. It is the individuals' way of affirming their own value, in terms of their private logic rather than common sense. All that would be necessary in such cases would be to win over the young people and give them courage.

We would cite many other examples. Consider a case of a girl, eleven years old, who was not liked at home. The other children were preferred, and she felt she was not wanted. She became peevish, aggressive, and disobedient. It is a simple case to analyze. The girl felt she was not appreciated, and at first she struggled against this, but then she lost hope. One day she stole something from a shop. For the Individual psychologist, stealing is not so much a crime as the enactment of a child's impulse unless one feels deprived. The girl's stealing was thus the result of her lack of affection at home and of her feeling of hopelessness. Children begin to steal when they feel deprived. Such feelings may not reflect the objective facts, but are nonetheless the psychological cause of their action.

Another case is that of an eight-year-old boy, an illegitimate, unattractive child who was living with foster parents. The foster parents did not take good care of him and did not discipline him. Sometimes the mother gave him sweets, and this was a bright spot in his life. The foster father was an old man, and the couple's own child, a girl, was the father's only pleasure in life. He pampered her continually and always brought home sweets for his little girl, but not for the boy. As a result the boy began to steal the sweets from her. He stole because he felt deprived and wanted to enrich himself. The father beat him for stealing, but the boy persisted. One might think that the boy showed courage in that he persisted in stealing in spite of the beatings, but that is not true—he always hoped to escape detection.

This is a case of a child never experiencing what it means to be a valued member of a family. He needs to be given the opportunity of living as a member of a community. When he learns to identify with others and to put himself in others' shoes, he will understand how his foster father feels when he sees him stealing and how the little girl feels when she discovers her sweets are gone. We see here again how lack of social feeling, lack of understanding, and lack of courage go together to form an inferiority complex.

XI
INTIMATE RELATIONSHIPS

The Importance of Preparation

THE RIGHT PREPARATION for intimate relationships, love, and marriage is first of all to be part of a community and to be socially well adjusted. Along with this, there should be a certain guidance of the sexual instincts, which are apparent from early childhood, to find their expression in marriage and a family.

All the necessary attitudes and inclinations for love and marriage can be found in the prototype formed in the first years of life. By observing the traits of the prototype we are able to put our finger on any difficulties that may appear later in adult life.

The problems that we meet in relationships, love, and marriage are of the same character as general social problems. There are the same difficulties and the same tasks, and it is a mistake to regard successful relationships and marriage as a potential paradise in which all things happen according to one's desires. There is always work to do, and this work must be accomplished with the interests of the partner constantly in mind.

More than the ordinary problems of social adjustment, marriage in particular requires an exceptional ability to identify oneself with another person. If few people are properly prepared nowadays for family life, it is because they have never learned to see with the eyes, hear with the ears, and feel with the heart of another person.

Much of our discussion in the previous chapters centered on the type of children who grow up interested only in themselves and not in others. Such children cannot be expected to change their character overnight with the onset of physical and sexual maturity. They will be unprepared for relationships in the same way and for the same reasons that they are unprepared for social life.

Social feeling is slow to develop and grow. Only those who are really trained in the direction of social interest from early childhood and who are always striving usefully will develop true social feeling. For this reason it is not particularly difficult to recognize whether a person is well prepared for life with a partner or not.

We need only remember what we have already observed: People must be courageous and have confidence in themselves to face the problems of life and go on to find solutions; they must have colleagues and friends and get along with their neighbors. People who do not have these traits are not to be regarded as prepared for relationships, love, and marriage. On the other hand, we may conclude that people are probably ready for such commitment if they have established themselves in a useful occupation and are progressing in it. We are judging their character by a small sign, but the sign is significant in that it indicates whether or not people have social feeling.

Equality of the Sexes

An understanding of the nature of social feeling shows us that the problems of love and marriage can be solved satisfactorily only on the basis of total equality between the sexes. This fundamental give-and-take is vitally important, much more important than whether one partner esteems the other. Love by itself does not settle the matter, for there are all kinds of love. It is only when there is a proper foundation of equality that love will take the right course and make marriage a success.

If either partner wishes to be the boss in a relationship, the results are likely to be fatal. Looking forward to a commitment with such a view in mind is not the right preparation, and subsequent events are likely to prove it. It is not possible to be a boss in a situation in which there is no place for a dominant partner. The marriage situation calls for an interest in the other person and an ability to put oneself in the other's place.

The Dynamics of Attraction

Let us turn now to the special preparation necessary for a committed relationship. This involves, as we have seen, the training of the social feeling in conjunction with the instinct of sexual attraction. From our childhood years on, we create in our own minds an ideal picture of a partner. For a boy, it is probable that his mother will provide the model for the ideal woman, and he will look for a similar type of partner. Sometimes there may be a state of unhappy tension between a boy and his mother, in which case he may look for a completely different type of partner. So close is the correspondence between a child's relation with his mother and the person he marries afterward that we can observe it in such little details as eye color, figure, hair color, and so on.

We know, too, that if a mother is domineering and suppresses her son, he may not want to act courageously when the time comes for becoming emotionally involved, for his sexual ideal is likely to be weak and obedient, or, if he is aggressive, he will fight and want to dominate his partner.

We can see how all the characteristics manifested in childhood are emphasized and magnified when people face the problem of love. We can imagine how people suffering from an inferiority complex will behave in sexual matters. Perhaps because they feel weak and inferior, they will express their feelings by always asking for support from other people. Often such types have the motherly character as an ideal. Or sometimes, by way of compensation for their inferiority, they may take the opposite direction in love and become arrogant and aggressive. Then they may select a stubborn or quarrelsome partner, finding it more honorable to be the conqueror in a difficult battle.

Neither sex can act successfully in this way. It is ridiculous to have the sexual relationship reduced to the satisfaction of an inferiority or superiority complex, and yet this happens frequently. If we look closely we see that in seeking a partner, many people are really looking for a victim. They do not understand that sexual relationships cannot be exploited for such ends. For if one person seeks to dominate, the other will do likewise. As a result, a shared life becomes impossible.

The observation that some people are attempting to satisfy their complexes illuminates certain peculiarities in their choice of a partner that are otherwise difficult to understand. It tells us why some people choose weak, sick, or old partners: They choose them because they believe they will have an easier time with them. Sometimes they choose someone already married; here it is a case of never wanting to make a commitment. Sometimes we find people falling in love with two people at the same time, because as I have already remarked, "two people are less than one."

We have seen how people who suffer from an inferiority complex change jobs, refuse to face problems, and often fail to finish things. When confronted with the problem of love they act similarly. Falling in love with a married person or with two people at once is a way of perpetuating habitual indecisiveness. There are other ways, too, such as overlong engagements that never result in marriage.

The Spoiled Child

Spoiled children show up in relationships and marriage true to type: They want to be pampered by their partners. Such a state of affairs may exist without danger in the early stages of a relationship or in the first years of marriage, but later it will bring about complications. We can imagine what happens when two such people develop a relationship. Both want to be pampered, and neither of them wants to be the one who pampers. It is as if they each stood around expecting something from the other and giving nothing. Both have the feeling that they are misunderstood.

When people feel misunderstood and thwarted, they feel inferior and want to escape. Such feelings are extremely bad in a relationship or marriage, particularly if a sense of hopelessness arises. When this happens, the desire for revenge begins to creep in; one person wants to disrupt the life of the other. The most common way to do this is to be unfaithful. Infidelity is often an act of vengeance. True, partners who are unfaithful always justify themselves by speaking about love and feelings, but we know the value of such feelings and sentiments: They always agree with the goal of superiority and should not be regarded as anything but excuses.

As an illustration we may take the case of a certain pampered woman. She married a man who had always felt in the shadow of his brother. The man was attracted by the mildness and sweetness of this woman, an only child, who in turn expected always to be appreciated and the center of attention. The marriage was quite happy until a child came along. We can predict what happened then: The wife still wanted to be the center of attention but was afraid that the child might take that position, and so she was not very happy. The husband, on the other hand, also wanted to be number one and was afraid that the child would usurp his place. As a result, husband and wife became suspicious of one another. They did not neglect the child and were quite good parents, but they were always expecting that their love for each other would decrease. Such a suspicion is dangerous, because if one starts to measure every word, every action, it is easy to find, or to appear to find, a decrease in affection. In this case, both parties found it.

The husband went on a holiday to Paris and enjoyed himself while his wife recuperated from childbirth and looked after the baby. He wrote exuberant letters from Paris, telling his wife what a good time he was having, how he was meeting all sorts of people, and so on. The wife began to feel neglected, became depressed, and soon began to suffer from agoraphobia. She could not go out alone anymore. When her husband returned he had to accompany her everywhere. On the surface at least, it would seem that she attained her goal and that she was now the center of attention. But nonetheless she had the feeling that if her agoraphobia disappeared, her husband would disappear, too, so she continued to suffer from agoraphobia.

During her illness she found a doctor who gave her considerable attention. While under his care she felt much better, and all the feelings of friendship she had she directed toward him. But when the doctor decided that she was better, he stopped seeing her. She wrote him a letter thanking him for all he had done for her, but he did not reply. From this time on, her illness became worse.

At this time she began to have ideas and fantasies about liaisons with other men in order to revenge herself upon her husband. However, her agoraphobia—her fear of going out alone—prevented her from being unfaithful to her husband.

Offering Advice

We see so many mistakes made in relationships and marriage that the question inevitably arises, "Is all this necessary?" We know that these mistakes originated in childhood, and we know, too, that it is possible to change mistaken life styles by recognizing the characteristics of the prototype. One wonders, therefore, whether it would not be possible to establish advisory bodies that could untangle relationship mistakes using the methods of Individual Psychology. Such organizations would consist of trained people who would understand how all the events in individuals' lives cohere and hang together and who would have the power of sympathetic identification with those seeking advice.

These organizations would not say, "You cannot agree, you quarrel continuously; therefore you should split up." For what use is splitting up? People often want to become involved or marry again, and often only continue the same life style as before. We sometimes see people who have broken up time and again, and still get involved in new relationships in which they simply repeat their mistakes. Such people might ask our advisory body whether their proposed marriage or relationship had in it any possibility of success. Or, they might consult it before separating.

Mistaken Attitudes

A number of small mistakes occur in a person's childhood, most of which do not seem important until she becomes involved in a committed relationship. For example, some people expect that they will be disappointed in life. There are children who are never happy and who are constantly in fear of being disappointed, who either feel that they have been displaced in the parental affections by another, or who have experienced an early difficulty that has made them superstitiously afraid that misfortune may recur. We can see that this fear and expectation of disappointment creates jealousy and suspicion in relationships and marriage.

Among women, there is a particular difficulty in that they may feel they are only playthings for men, and that men are always unfaithful. It is unlikely that people with views like this will be able to sustain a happy relationship. Happiness is impossible if one party has the fixed idea that the other is likely to be unfaithful.

From the way in which people seek advice on love, one would judge that it is generally regarded as the most important task of life. From the point of view of Individual Psychology, however, it is not the most important task, although its importance is not to be undervalued. For Individual Psychology, no single task in life is more important than another. If people overemphasize the task of love and marriage, they destroy the harmony of life.

Perhaps the reason why love is given such undue importance in many people's minds is that, unlike other tasks, it is a topic on which we do not receive any education. As we have said, there are three great tasks of life. The first, the social question, involves our behavior with others, and we are taught from the first day of our lives how to act in the company of others. We learn these things quite early. Likewise, we have courses of training to prepare us for our careers. We have teachers to instruct us in the various arts, and we have books that tell us what to do. But where are the books that tell us how to prepare for an intimate relationship? To be sure, there are a great many dealing with love stories, but we find few books dealing with happy marriages.

Love and marriage have had bad press from the beginning. If we look at the Bible, we will find there the story that a woman began all the trouble, and ever since then men and women have always experienced problems in their love lives.

Our educational system could certainly be much improved. It would be wise to train girls and boys better in the roles of marriage, but train them both in such a way that they feel equal.

That women often feel inferior proves that, in this particular, our culture has failed. Women often want to overcome others and train themselves more than is necessary, becoming self-centered. In the future, women must be taught to develop more social interest and not to seek benefit exclusively for themselves. But to do this, we must first banish superstitions regarding the privileges of men.

Danger Signs

Let us take an example to show how poorly prepared for committed relationships some people are. A young man was dancing at a party with his pretty fiancee. He happened to drop his glasses, and to the utter amazement of the other guests, he almost knocked the girl down in order to grab them. When a friend asked him, "What on earth were you doing?" he replied, "I could not let her break my glasses." We can see that this young man was not prepared for marriage, and indeed the marriage did not take place. Later in life he visited the doctor and said he was suffering from depression, as is often the case with people who are too interested in themselves.

There are a thousand signs by which one can gauge whether or not a person is prepared for marriage. One should not trust a person in love who arrives late for a date without an adequate excuse. Such action shows a hesitating attitude and may be a sign of lack of preparation for the problems of life. It is also a sign of lack of preparation if one half of a couple always wants to educate the other or always needs to criticize. To be oversensitive is a bad sign, since it indicates an inferiority complex. People who have no friends and do not mix well in society are not well prepared for an emotional life. Delay in choosing a career is also not a good sign. Pessimistic people are also ill-fitted, because pessimism betrays a lack of courage to face situations.

Despite this list of undesirables it should not be so difficult to choose the right person, or rather to choose a person along the right lines. We cannot expect to find an ideal person, and indeed, if we see someone searching for an ideal partner and never finding that partner, we may be sure that such a person is suffering from chronic hesitance.

Marriage as a Social Task

In conclusion, let me repeat that the questions of relationships, love, and marriage can be solved only by socially adjusted people. Mistakes are, in the majority of cases, due to lack of social feeling, and these mistakes can be obviated only if people change.

A relationship is a task for two. We are educated, however, either for tasks that can be performed alone or for ones that rely on groups of people—never for a task that takes two. But despite our lack of education, relationships and marriage can be handled properly if the partners recognize the mistakes in their character and approach things in a spirit of equality.

It is almost unnecessary to add that the highest form of relationship is monogamy. There are many people who claim on pseudo-scientific grounds that polygamy is better adapted to human nature, but this cannot be accepted, because in our culture love and marriage are social tasks. We do not have relationships for our private good only, but indirectly for the social good. In the last analysis, marriage is for the sake of the race.

XII
SEXUALITY AND SEXUAL PROBLEMS

Fact and Superstition

We discussed the normal problems of relationships, love, and marriage in the preceding chapter. We turn now to a more specific area of the same general question: problems of sexuality and their bearing upon real or imagined abnormalities. We have already seen that most people are less well prepared and less well trained for successful sexual relationships than for other life skills. In the whole question of human sexuality, it is extraordinary how many superstitions still need to be laid to rest.

The most common superstition concerns inherited characteristics—the belief that there are degrees of sexuality that are of genetic origin and cannot change. The concept of inheritance is easily used as an excuse or a subterfuge to avoid efforts at improvement. It is necessary, therefore, to be wary of some of the opinions that are advanced on behalf of science, which are often taken too seriously by the average layperson. Scientists give only the results of their studies and do not discuss the possible effects of training and education or adverse environmental factors.

Childhood Sexuality

Sexuality manifests itself very early in life. Any caregiver or parent who observes closely enough can see that in the first days of birth there are already certain sexual impulses. This display of sexuality is much more dependent upon environment than one might expect, however. When children begin to express themselves sexually, parents should find ways to distract them. Often, however, they do not provide the right type of distraction. We have seen that children may develop a strong interest in other organs of the body if natural development is impaired or if attitudes are mistaken, and the sex organs are no exception. But if one begins early enough it is possible to train children correctly.

In general, some sexual expression in childhood is quite normal, and we should not be concerned by it. Our policy should therefore be one of watching and waiting, and standing by to see that sexual expression does not develop in an unhealthy direction.

There is a tendency to attribute to inherited characteristics what is really the result of self-training during childhood. Sometimes this very act of self-training is regarded as an inherited characteristic, so that if children happen to be more interested in their own sex than in the other sex, this is considered to be a factor in their genetic makeup. But this is a tendency that develops from day to day. Sometimes children or adults show signs of sexual perversion, and here again many people believe this to be genetic. But if this is the case, why do such people train themselves? Why do they dream about and rehearse their actions?

Some people's sexual development stops at a certain age, and this fact can be explained along the lines of Individual Psychology. There are, for example, those who fear defeat because they have an inferiority complex, and in a case of this kind we note exaggerations that suggest overstressed sexuality. Such people may possess greater sexual potency.

This type of development may be specially stimulated by the environment. We know how pictures, books, films, or certain social contacts tend to overstress the sex drive. In the modern world one may say that almost everything tends to develop an exaggerated interest in sex. It is unnecessary to play down the great importance of these natural drives and of the part they play in love, marriage, and procreation, in order to assert that sex is overemphasized these days.

It is the exaggeration of sexuality that parents must guard against. Too often parents pay too much attention to the first manifestations of sexuality in childhood and thereby tend to make the child overvalue their significance. They are always talking to the child about these matters and punishing him or her. Now, we know that many children like to be the center of attention, and hence it is frequently the case that children continue in these habits precisely because they are scolded for them. It is better not to stress the subject with children, but to treat the matter like any other, and show children that one is not preoccupied with these things. Parents often express their affection for a child in kisses, embraces, and so on. Such things are healthy but should not be inappropriately overdone, because a pampered child does not develop well sexually.

The Life Style and Sexuality

Many doctors and psychologists believe that the development of sexuality is the basis for the development of the whole mind and psyche, as well as for all physical development. In my view this is not true. On the contrary, the whole form and development of sexuality is dependent upon the personality—the life style and the prototype.

Thus, for example, if we know that a child expresses his or her sexuality in a certain way, or that another child suppresses it, we may guess what will happen to both of them in their adult life. If we know that the child always wants to be the center of attention and to be the boss, then he or she will also develop sexually so as to dominate and be the center of attention.

Many people believe that they are superior and dominant when they express their sexual instincts polygamously. They therefore have sexual relationships with many partners, and it is easy to see that they deliberately overstress their sexual desires for psychological reasons. The resultant illusion that they are conquerors serves as a compensation for an inferiority complex.

It is the inferiority complex that is at the core of sexual abnormalities.

A person who suffers from an inferiority complex is always looking for the easiest way out, and sometimes finds this by excluding most aspects of life and exaggerating sexuality.

In children we often find this tendency among those who crave the attention of others. They monopolize their parents' and teachers' attention by creating difficulties for them, and later in life they try to dominate others and wish to be sexually superior. Such children grow up confusing sexual desire with the desire for conquest and superiority. Sometimes, in the course of their exclusion of some of the possibilities and problems of life, they may entirely exclude the other sex and self-train for homosexuality.[1] An overstressed sexuality is often used as an insurance against having to face the problem of living out a conventional sex life.

We can understand all this only if we understand a person's life style. These people want to have much attention paid to them and yet believe themselves incapable of sufficiently interesting the other sex. Their inferiority complex in regard to the other sex may be traced back to childhood. For instance, if a boy found the behavior of girls in the family and the behavior of his mother more attractive than his own, he may have come to believe that he would never have the power to interest women. Other individuals may admire the other sex so much that they begin to imitate them. Thus we may see men who want to be like women and women who want to be like men.

A Criminal Case

There is a case of a man accused of sadism and of sexual acts against children that illustrates the formation of the tendencies we have been discussing. Inquiring into his development, we learn that he had a dominant mother who was always criticizing him. Despite this, he developed into a good and intelligent pupil at school, but his mother

1. Again, homosexuality is seen today as unlikely to be a choice but biologically predisposed.

was never satisfied with his success. For this reason he wanted to exclude his mother from his affections and was not interested in her, but occupied himself with his father.

We can see how such a child might form the idea that women are severe and hypercritical and that contact with them is not to be made for pleasure but only out of necessity. In this way he came to exclude the other sex from his life. But he was also of the type who becomes sexually aroused when afraid. Suffering from anxiety and being thus stimulated, this type of person may later in life like to punish or torture himself, or see a child tortured, or just imagine himself or another being tortured. He will find sexual satisfaction only in the course of these real or imaginary tortures.

The case of this man indicates the drastic results of the wrong kind of training. The man never understood the reasons behind his habits, or if he did he only saw them when it was too late. Of course it is difficult to train a person properly at the age of twenty-five or thirty. The right time is early childhood.

But in childhood, psychological relations with the parents complicate matters. It is curious to see how bad sexual training results from the psychological conflict between child and parent. An aggressive child, especially in the period of adolescence, may abuse sexuality with the deliberate intention of hurting his parents. Boys and girls have been known to have sex just after a fight with their parents. Children use these means to revenge themselves on their parents, particularly when they see that their parents are sensitive on this subject. An aggressive child particularly may well take this point of attack. The only way such tactics can be avoided is to make all children responsible for themselves, so that they should not believe that it is the parents' interest alone that is at stake, but their own as well.

Besides the influence of childhood environment as reflected in the life style, the political and economic conditions in a country have their influence on sexuality. Certain conditions create a social style that can be very contagious. One finds an exaggeration of sexuality during a revolution or other extreme social disturbance, and it is of course notorious that in wartime there is widespread recourse to sensuality because life seems precarious and worthless.

Sexual Excess

It has been remarked that humans are the only animals that eat when they are not hungry, drink when they are not thirsty, and have sexual relations at all times. The overindulgence of the sexual instinct is similar to the overindulgence of other urges. When any appetite is overindulged and any interest is overdeveloped, this interferes with the harmony of life. Psychologists' records are full of cases where people develop interests or appetites to the point at which they become a compulsion. We are familiar with cases of misers who overstress the importance of money, but there are also people who think cleanliness is all-important. They put washing ahead of all other activities and even spend the whole day and half the night washing. Then there are people who insist on the paramount importance of eating. They eat all day long, are interested only in food, and talk about nothing but eating.

The cases of sexual excess are precisely the same. They lead to an imbalance in the harmony of human activity and inevitably drag the whole life style toward useless activities.

In the proper training of the sexual instincts, sexual drives should be harnessed to a useful goal in which the whole of our character is expressed. If the goal is properly chosen, neither sexuality nor any other single aspect of life will be overemphasized.

On the other hand, while it is important that all appetites and interests are controlled and harmonized, there is danger in complete suppression of any of them. Just as in the matter of food, when people diet to excess their minds and bodies suffer, so, too, in the matter of sex, complete abstinence is undesirable.

What this implies is that in a normal life style, sex will find its proper expression. It does not mean that we can overcome neuroses, which are the marks of an unbalanced life style, merely by free, unrestrained sexual expression. The belief, so widely propagated, that a suppressed libido is the cause of neurosis is untrue. Rather it is the other way around: Neurotic people do not find their proper sexual expression.

One meets people who have been advised to give free rein to their sexual instincts and who have followed that advice, only to make their condition worse. This happens because such people fail to integrate their sexual lives with socially useful goals, which is the only thing that can improve their neurotic condition. The expression of the sexual instinct alone does not cure the neurosis, for the neurosis is a disease of the life style, and it can be cured only by ministering to the life style.

For the Individual psychologist, all this is so clear that he does not hesitate to say a happy marriage or committed partnership is the only satisfactory solution for sexual problems. A neurotic does not look favorably on such a solution, because a neurotic is always a coward and not well prepared for social life. Similarly, people who overstress sexuality, who talk of polygamy and of open relationships or trial marriage, are trying to escape the social solution to the question of sex. They have no resources for solving the problem of social adjustment on the basis of cooperation between husband and wife, and they dream of escape through the use of some new formula. Often, however, the road that seems the most difficult is in fact the most direct.

XIII

CONCLUSION

It is time to conclude our survey. The method of Individual Psychology begins and ends with the problem of inferiority, which is the basis for human striving and success. On the other hand, the sense of inferiority is also the basis for all our problems of psychological maladjustment. When an individual does not find a proper concrete goal of superiority, an inferiority complex results, leading to a desire for escape. This desire for escape is expressed in a superiority complex, which is nothing more than a useless, vain goal offering the satisfaction of false success.

These are the dynamics of psychological life. We know that mistakes in the functioning of the psyche are more harmful at certain times than at others. We know that the life style crystallizes in tendencies formed in childhood—in the prototype that develops by the age of four or five. And this being so, the whole burden of encouraging a healthy psychological life rests on proper childhood guidance, where the principal aim should be the cultivation of proper social feeling in terms of useful and healthy goals. It is only by training children to fit in with the social scheme that the natural human sense of inferiority is properly harnessed and prevented from engendering either an inferiority or a superiority complex.

Social adjustment is the other side of the coin of the inferiority problem. It is because the individual is inferior and weak that we find human beings living together in society. Social interest and cooperation are, therefore, the salvation of the individual.

GLOSSARY OF KEY TERMS

Individual Psychology: The study of the individual as an indivisible whole, as a unitary, goal-directed self, which in the normal, healthy state is a full member of society and a participant in human relationships.

Inferiority complex: Feelings of inferiority or inadequacy that produce stress, psychological evasions, and a compensatory drive toward an illusory sense of superiority.

Life style: A key concept in Individual Psychology. The complex of an individual's personal philosophy, beliefs, and characteristic approach to life, and the unifying feature of the individual's personality. The life style represents an individual's creative response to early experiences, which in turn influences all her perceptions of herself and the world, and thus her emotions, motives, and actions. It was in this present work that Adler formally introduced the term *life style* instead of the earlier expressions such as *guiding line* and *life plan.*

Masculine protest: A reaction, by either sex, to the prejudices of our society about masculinity and femininity. A man's behavior may constitute a protest against the demands made on him by the myths of male superiority. A woman's may be a protest against the denigration of femininity and the limitations placed on women.

Misguided behavior: An attempt to compensate for a feeling of inadequacy or insecurity indirectly, based on a mistaken "private logic."

Organ inferiority: A physical defect or weakness that often leads to compensatory behavior.

Other sex: Adler's term for "opposite sex," emphasizing that male and female are not opposite but complementary.

Pampering: Overindulgence or overprotectiveness of children, stunting the development of their self-reliance, courage, responsibility, and capacity for cooperation with others.

Prototype: An early form of the life style, *prototype* is a term no longer used by Individual Psychologists.

Psyche: The mind; the whole personality—both conscious and unconscious—which directs personal drives, gives significance to perceptions and sensations, and originates needs and goals.

Social interest (or social feeling): Community spirit; the sense of human fellowship and identity with the whole of humanity that entails positive social relationships. For Adler, these relationships should incorporate equality, reciprocity, and cooperation if they are to be constructive and healthy. Social interest begins with the ability to empathize with a fellow human being and leads to the striving for an ideal community based on cooperation and personal equality. This concept is integral to Adler's view of the individual as a social being.

Tasks of life: The three broad areas of human experience that each individual must confront: the tasks of pursuing a socially useful profession or occupation, of building fruitful human relationships, and of fulfilling one's role in love, marriage, and family life.

SELECT BIBLIOGRAPHY

Books by Alfred Adler:

The Case of Miss R: The Interpretation of a Life Story. New York: Greenberg, 1929.

The Education of Children. Chicago: Regnery Publishing, 1970.

The Neurotic Constitution. New York: Arno Press, 1974.

The Pattern of Life. New York: Rinehart and Company, 1930.

The Practice and Theory of Individual Psychology. New York: Harcourt, Brace and Company, 1927.

Problems of Neurosis: A Book of Case Histories. New York: Harper Torchbooks, 1964.

Social Interest: A Challenge to Mankind. New York: Capricorn Books, 1964.

Understanding Human Nature. Oxford: Oneworld Publications, 1992; Center City, Minn.: Hazelden, 1998.

What Life Could Mean to You. Oxford: Oneworld Publications, 1992; Center City, Minn.: Hazelden, 1998.

Books about Alfred Adler and His Work:

Adlerian Counseling and Psychotherapy. D. C. Dinkmeyer, D. C. Dinkmeyer Jr., and L. Sperry. Columbus: Merrill Publishing Company, 1987.

Alfred Adler: A Portrait from Life. P. Bottome. New York: Vanguard, 1957.

Alfred Adler: The Man and His Work. H. Orgler. New York: Capricorn Books, 1965.

The Freud-Adler Controversy. Handelbauer. Oxford: Oneworld Publications, 1997.

Fundamentals of Adlerian Psychology. Rudolf Dreikurs. Chicago: Alfred Adler Institute, 1953.

The Individual Psychology of Alfred Adler: A Systematic Presentation in Selection from His Writings. L. Heinz and Rowena R. Ansbacher, eds. New York: Harper Touchbooks, 1964.

Individual Psychology: Theory and Practice. Guy J. Manaster and Raymond Corsini. Chicago: Adler School of Professional Psychology, 1982.

INDEX

ABOUT THE AUTHOR AND EDITOR

Alfred Adler (1870–1937) was born in a suburb of Vienna, the son of a Jewish grain merchant. He became a medical doctor and was one of the first to take a serious interest in the theories of Sigmund Freud. Adler recognized that the theories opened a new phase in the development of psychiatry and psychology. He joined Freud's discussion group and in 1910 became president of the Vienna Psychoanalytic Society. Shortly afterward, the divergence between his views and those of Freud and Carl Jung led to his resignation.

Clearly Adler's onetime colleague deeply influenced his work, but from the beginning Adler had an independent approach to formulating the problems of human psychology and finding solutions to them. In 1912 he formed the Society for Individual Psychology, which stressed the importance of taking a broad and responsive view of the human personality rather than adherence to the Freudians' strict scientific principles.

After serving as a medical doctor in the First World War, Adler founded a system of child-guidance clinics that spread throughout Europe. He was personally involved in training teachers, social workers, doctors, and psychiatrists in his techniques. His lecture tours of the United States became more frequent, and in 1935 he fled an increasingly anti-Semitic Europe to settle in America. He died in 1937 while on a lecture tour of Scotland. Adler's name is bracketed with those of Freud and Jung as one of the three great fathers of modern psychotherapy.

Colin Brett is an accredited Adlerian counselor and former training officer of the Adlerian Society of Great Britain. He currently works as a freelance management consultant and Adlerian counselor trainer in both Great Britain and South Africa. He is the translator of Alfred Adler's *Understanding Human Nature* and the editor of *What Life Could Mean to You,* both published by Oneworld Publications, 1992, and in North America by Hazelden, 1998.

HAZELDEN INFORMATION AND EDUCATIONAL SERVICES is a division of the Hazelden Foundation, a not-for-profit organization. Since 1949, Hazelden has been a leader in promoting the dignity and treatment of people afflicted with the disease of chemical dependency.

The mission of the foundation is to improve the quality of life for individuals, families, and communities by providing a national continuum of information, education, and recovery services that are widely accessible; to advance the field through research and training; and to improve our quality and effectiveness through continuous improvement and innovation.

Stemming from that, the mission of this division is to provide quality information and support to people wherever they may be in their personal journey—from education and early intervention, through treatment and recovery, to personal and spiritual growth.

Although our treatment programs do not necessarily use everything Hazelden publishes, our bibliotherapeutic materials support our mission and the Twelve Step philosophy upon which it is based. We encourage your comments and feedback.

The headquarters of the Hazelden Foundation are in Center City, Minnesota. Additional treatment facilities are located in Chicago, Illinois; New York, New York; Plymouth, Minnesota; St. Paul, Minnesota; and West Palm Beach, Florida. At these sites, we provide a continuum of care for men and women of all ages. Our Plymouth facility is designed specifically for youth and families.

For more information on Hazelden, please call **1-800-257-7800**. Or you may access our World Wide Web site on the Internet at **http://www.hazelden.org**.